HOUSE OF LORDS
HOUSE OF COMMONS

SI

CW00572532

JOINT COMMITTEE ON FINANCIAL SERVICES AND MARKETS

Second Report

DRAFT FINANCIAL SERVICES AND MARKETS BILL

Parts V, VI and XII in relation to the European Convention on Human Rights

Report, together with the Proceedings of the Committee, Minutes of Evidence and Appendices

Ordered by The House of Lords *to be printed*
27 May 1999

Ordered by The House of Commons *to be printed*
27 May 1999, pursuant to Standing Order No. 137

LONDON: THE STATIONERY OFFICE

HL Paper 66
HC 465

ORDERS OF REFERENCE

HOUSE OF LORDS

Tuesday 2 March 1999

Financial Services and Markets—It was moved by the Chairman of Committees that the Commons message of yesterday be now considered and that a Select Committee of eight Lords be appointed to join with the Committee appointed by the Commons, as the Joint Committee on Financial Services and Markets, to report on the consultative document on the draft financial services and markets bill presented by Her Majesty's Command on 21st December 1998 and any further draft of the bill which may be laid upon the Table of both Houses by a Minister of the Crown;

That, as proposed by the Committee of Selection, the following Lords be named of the Committee:

L. Burns	L. Montague of Oxford
L. Eatwell	L. Poole
L. Fraser of Carmyllie	L. Taverne
L. Haskel	V. Trenchard

That the Committee have power to agree with the Commons in the appointment of a Chairman;
That the Committee have leave to report from time to time;
That the Committee have power to appoint specialist advisers;
That the Committee have power to adjourn from place to place within the United Kingdom;
That the minutes of evidence taken before the Committee from time to time shall, if the Committee think fit, be printed and delivered out;
That the Committee shall report by 30th April 1999;
and that the Committee do meet with the Committee appointed by the Commons this day at half past four o'clock in Committee Room 3A;
the motion was agreed to and a message was ordered to be sent to the Commons to acquaint them therewith.

Wednesday 28 April 1999

Financial Services and Markets—It was moved by the Baroness Jay of Paddington that this House do concur with the Commons in the Order set out in their message of yesterday that it be an Instruction to the Joint Committee on Financial Services and Markets that it report by 27th May 1999 on Parts V (employment in regulated activities), VI (civil fines for market abuse) and XII (disciplinary measures) of the draft bill in relation to the European Convention on Human Rights; the motion was agreed to (see division list) and a message was ordered to be sent to the Commons to acquaint them therewith.

HOUSE OF COMMONS

Friday 26 February 1999

Financial Services and Markets,—*Ordered,* That a Select Committee of eight Members be appointed to join with a committee to be appointed by the Lords, to be the Joint Committee on Financial Services and Markets, to report on the consultative document on the draft Financial Services and Markets Bill presented by Her Majesty's Command on 21st December 1998 and any further draft of the Bill which may be laid upon the Table of both Houses by a Minister of the Crown;

Ordered, That three be the quorum of the Committee;
Ordered, That the Committee shall have power—
  (i)   to send for persons, papers and records;

HOUSE OF LORDS
HOUSE OF COMMONS

SESSION 1998–99

JOINT COMMITTEE ON FINANCIAL SERVICES AND MARKETS

Second Report

DRAFT FINANCIAL SERVICES AND MARKETS BILL

Parts V, VI and XII in relation to the European Convention on Human Rights

Report, together with the Proceedings of the Committee, Minutes of Evidence and Appendices

Ordered by The House of Lords *to be printed*
27 May 1999

Ordered by The House of Commons *to be printed*
27 May 1999, pursuant to Standing Order No. 137

LONDON: THE STATIONERY OFFICE

HL Paper 66
HC 465

(ii)   to sit notwithstanding any adjournment of the House;

(iii) to report from time to time;

(iv) to appoint specialist advisers;

(v)   to adjourn from place to place within the United Kingdom;

(vi) to communicate to any Select Committee appointed by either House its evidence and any documents of common interest;

Ordered, That the Committee shall report by 30th April 1999;

Ordered, That Mr Nigel Beard, Mrs Liz Blackman, Dr Vincent Cable, Mr David Heathcoat-Amory, Mr David Kidney, Mr Tim Loughton, Mr James Plaskitt and Mr Barry Sheerman be members of the Committee.—(*Mr Jim Dowd.*)

Tuesday 27 April 1999

Financial Services and Markets,—*Ordered,* That it be an Instruction to the Joint Committee on Financial Services and Markets that it report by 27th May 1999 on Parts V (employment in regulated activities), VI (civil fines for market abuse) and XII (disciplinary measures) of the draft bill in relation to the European Convention on Human Rights.—(*Mr Robert Ainsworth.*)

TABLE OF CONTENTS

Page

SECOND REPORT

The Joint Committee on Financial Services and Markets has agreed to the following Report:—

DRAFT FINANCIAL SERVICES AND MARKETS BILL

Parts V, VI and XII in relation to the European Convention on Human Rights

Introduction

1. In our First Report,[1] we raised concerns about the compatibility of parts of the Government's draft Financial Services and Markets Bill with the European Convention on Human Rights (ECHR). We have been instructed by the two Houses[2] to report again on these matters, in respect of three parts of the draft Bill: Parts V and XII, giving the Financial Services Authority (FSA) powers of discipline and enforcement over approved persons (i.e. individuals working in positions of responsibility in financial services) and authorised persons (mostly financial service businesses); and Part VI, giving the FSA powers against market abuse.

2. The main concern about these parts of the draft Bill expressed in our First Report was as follows. The regimes which they put in place are expressed as civil justice regimes. However we found it to be arguable, and in the case of Part VI strongly arguable, that the courts would find them to be of the nature of criminal justice for ECHR purposes. The ECHR sets standards for all judicial proceedings; but for criminal proceedings it requires a set of extra safeguards—notably privilege against self-incrimination, a right to free legal assistance where appropriate, and a high degree of clarity as to what behaviour is forbidden. We found Parts V, VI and XII of the draft Bill to be lacking in these respects. This would lay proceedings under those Parts open to challenge in the courts,[3] and might even result in the legislation being declared incompatible with the Convention.

3. We recommended that the Government should publish its reasoned view on these matters as soon as possible, and it did so on 14th May.[4] Its position with regard to FSA disciplinary proceedings for authorised and approved persons (Parts V and XII) is unchanged: it considers that the courts will treat these as civil proceedings in ECHR terms. However it now recognises a real possibility that proceedings for a fine for market abuse (under Part VI) might be classified as criminal. It has therefore decided to provide additional safeguards for the person proceeded against: compelled statements will not be able to be used against the person who made them, and subsidised legal assistance will be available where appropriate. The Government also proposes measures to give greater certainty, though it considers that the provisions in the draft Bill are sufficient for ECHR purposes in this respect.

4. We welcome the Government's willingness to listen and respond to argument on these matters. It seems to us to be a powerful vindication of pre-legislative scrutiny, and it will make for more informed debate on the Bill. We especially commend the Government for its response to concerns about the market abuse regime. The additional safeguards may make it harder for the FSA to launch proceedings. However they will make it more likely that proceedings launched will withstand challenge on human rights grounds; and they will increase the confidence of the regulated community that they will receive fair treatment. Rough justice may get results in the short term; but in the long run it breeds disaffection and resentment, and is not sustainable.

---

[1] HL Paper 50, HC 328, published 29th April. Our original terms of reference were "to report on the consultative document on the draft financial services and markets bill presented by Her Majesty's Command on 21st December 1998 and any further draft of the bill which may be laid upon the Table of both Houses by a Minister of the Crown".

[2] House of Commons 27th April, House of Lords 28th April.

[3] The UK courts already have regard to ECHR principles, which to a great extent reflect long-standing principles of UK law; and a party who has exhausted his remedies in the UK may appeal to the European Court of Human Rights in Strasbourg. After the commencement of the Human Rights Act 1998, which, the Government has recently announced, will be on 2nd October 2000, the UK courts will be able to apply the ECHR directly.

[4] Evidence, p 1.

5. Running through our deliberations has been the need to strike a balance between the competing demands of fairness and effectiveness. As Lord Steyn, one of the Lords of Appeal in Ordinary ("Law Lords"), puts it,[5] "the new regulatory system must be just and must protect Convention rights, but...in order to serve the interests of the public it must be effective". With regard to disciplinary proceedings, the Government's position is pragmatic, and in principle we agree with this approach. Writing into the Bill the full panoply of criminal justice safeguards for every disciplinary action, however minor, would imperil the effectiveness of the whole regulatory regime. We remain concerned, however, that incorporating none of them, even for actions where severe penalties are at stake, entails a risk of defeat in court. We discuss below ways in which this risk might be reduced.

6. We are instructed to report by 27th May; our proceedings have therefore been very limited. We have taken oral evidence from the Economic Secretary to the Treasury, Patricia Hewitt MP, and her legal advisers, Sydney Kentridge QC and James Eadie; and we have received a small amount of written evidence.[6] We are grateful to all our witnesses, who have necessarily had to respond swiftly and at very short notice. We record again our thanks to our Specialist Advisers: Dr Eilís Ferran of Cambridge University, Professor David Llewellyn of Loughborough University, and Professor Alan Page of Dundee University.

7. The Annex contains revised versions of Tables I-III from our First Report, which analyse the various forms of enforcement power conferred on the FSA by Parts V, VI and XII of the draft Bill.

Discipline and Enforcement

8. It is common ground that four factors fall to be taken into account in determining whether proceedings are civil or criminal for ECHR purposes.[7] They are:

- Characterisation in domestic law (not conclusive).

- Nature of conduct: does it overlap with criminal law?

- Whether the regime applies to everyone (which would suggest a criminal-type regime), or only to a particular group subject to special regulation (which would suggest a civil regime).

- Nature and level of penalty.

9. The Government maintains that all FSA disciplinary proceedings will be classed as civil in ECHR terms. Its main reason is that the scope of the regime is limited to a defined set of persons who are part of a regulated community which they have chosen to join. Mr Kentridge gave us a list of cases where the European Court of Human Rights has treated as civil the disciplinary proceedings of the regulators of various professions and occupations.[8] The list included some regulators operating on a contractual and self-regulating basis, like the Investment Management Regulatory Organisation (IMRO, which is now part of the FSA); but it also included statutory regulators like the FSA, such as the General Medical Council (GMC).[9]

10. Lord Lester of Herne Hill QC[10] considers that the Government's approach is "too sweeping…, and leaves scope for considerable legal uncertainty and a real risk of a successful legal challenge in a particular case". He offers two arguments, both of which we put to the Minister.

[5] Appendix 3.
[6] See Appendices 1 to 9.
[7] Evidence, p 2, para. 9; Lester Annexes C and D to First Report.
[8] Q 5.
[9] Q 12.
[10] Appendix 2.

11. First, in some cases the conduct proceeded against may be in the nature of criminal conduct. Mr Kentridge answered this argument by citing the European Court case of *Wickramsinghe*, a doctor.[11] In this case, the conduct which was the subject of disciplinary proceedings (before the UK General Medical Council) was itself clearly criminal (indecent assault); yet the court held the GMC's proceedings in respect of that conduct to be civil for ECHR purposes. Lord Lester cited the case of *Oury* in France; Mr Kentridge replied that in that case the conduct in question was closer to market abuse than to a disciplinary matter.[12]

12. Secondly, Lord Lester observed that, in some cases, the penalty at stake will be "drastic fines with a dominantly punitive, rather than compensatory or restitutionary purpose".[13] The Minister and Mr Kentridge admitted that fines are punitive and deterrent in nature.[14] But they insisted that the possibility of a fine did not make the regime criminal in ECHR terms; they cited the case of *Brown*, a UK solicitor fined £10,000 by the Law Society, whose appeal to Strasbourg on the ground that he had been subjected to criminal justice without the Convention safeguards was turned down. They observed that, in disciplinary proceedings, a fine may be more lenient than other possible sanctions, such as striking-off.

13. Lord Steyn[15] recognises the force of Lord Lester's arguments, but is of the view that "it is likely that the courts will generally speaking treat the disciplinary system as involving civil proceedings". But where the disciplinary matters closely overlap serious species of market abuse he regards the position as "entirely open."

14. It is not for us to prejudge the view of the courts on these conflicting legal arguments. Ministers are evidently satisfied that their case is strong enough to warrant a statement under s.19 of the Human Rights Act 1998 that the Bill is compatible with the ECHR.[16] However, on the evidence before us, there remains a possibility that, in particular circumstances, the courts will hold disciplinary proceedings under the legislation to be criminal proceedings in ECHR terms. This might arise for any of the following reasons:

- The nature of the conduct in question may overlap with the criminal offences of insider dealing and misleading the markets, or with the wider market abuse regime which, the Government has conceded, may be found to be criminal.

- The regime will apply only to individuals and firms working in financial services; and the Government makes much of the analogy with professions such as law and medicine. However this analogy is not altogether clear-cut; and, although there is substantial practitioner input into the work of the FSA, it will in fact be a body of a very different character from the General Medical Council, the Law Society, etc.

- Finally, the nature of the penalty, whether a fine, public censure or withdrawal of authorisation, will in some cases be both severe and punitive, as both the FSA and the Government admit.[17] The Government seeks to distinguish between sanctions whose primary purpose is punishment and those which are primarily "protective". We are not wholly convinced by this distinction, since the criminal justice system itself may be said to have as its prime purpose the protection of society by the punishment and deterrence of crime.

15. We recommend that the Government should give this matter further thought, and we offer three possibilities for its consideration.

---

[11]Q 5.

[12]Q 13. See LIBA, Appendix 9, para 13.

[13]Appendix 2.

[14]QQ 2-7.

[15]Appendix 3.

[16]For an account of the basis on which these statements are being made, see House of Lords *Hansard* 5th May 1999, col. WA92. Ministers will not normally provide written reasons, as they have in this case: Lords *Hansard* 19th May, col. WA 35.

[17]CP 17, paragraphs 102–110; Q4.

16. First, some of our witnesses suggest that it may be possible to draw a line in the Bill itself between disciplinary cases which might fall into the criminal category, and those which clearly would not.[18] For cases on the criminal side of the line, use of compelled statements would be restricted; subsidised legal assistance would be available; and the FSA would be advised to consider carefully before launching proceedings on the basis of breach only of a general Principle, rather than a detailed rule, lest they fail the foreseeability test of ECHR Article 7. This might be considered a small price to pay, to avoid defeat on human rights grounds in an important case. However we recognise that establishing appropriate statutory criteria for determining in advance which side of the line a particular case falls would not be easy, and would be bound to reduce the flexibility of the regime.

17. Alternatively, the Bill might provide for the FSA to apply criminal justice safeguards in disciplinary actions when it considers it appropriate to do so. This would allow more flexibility than writing a dividing line into the Bill, and it would allow practice to evolve in line with case law without a need for further legislation. As a public body, the FSA would of course be required to exercise this discretion reasonably and in accordance with the ECHR. Nothing in the Bill as presently drafted would prevent the FSA from proceeding as if the criminal justice safeguards applied—at least as regards privilege against self-incrimination; therefore this proposal might be seen as a clarification of the Government's proposals rather than a substantive change.

18. Finally, we would observe that the FSA's power to impose unlimited fines would look less like a criminal sanction if it were qualified in some way in the Bill. As it is, Clause 141 requires the FSA to publish a policy on fines and to abide by it, but lays down none of the content of that policy. In our First Report[19] we recommended against putting an upper limit on FSA fines, and we remain of this view. However in *Consultation Paper 17* published in December, the FSA indicated that it envisaged setting fines with regard to, among other things, the nature of the offence, the profit made (or loss avoided) by the offender, and the offender's resources.[20] We suggest that a requirement along these lines might be written into the Bill. Requiring the amount of the fine to be related to the offender's resources could arguably be characterised as retributive. However, **we recommend that the Bill should require, at least, that in setting the amount of any fine regard should be had to the mischief achieved or intended, and to whether the offender is an individual or a firm.**

Market Abuse

19. As noted above, the Government has announced a series of changes to Part VI of the Bill, the market abuse regime, to increase certainty and reduce the chance of successful legal challenge on ECHR grounds. These changes meet many of the points made in our First Report. We consider them in turn.

COMPELLED EVIDENCE

20. First, and most significantly for the FSA as it seeks to enforce the regime, statements which the FSA compel a person to make will not be able to be used against him in proceedings. The Minister observed that this would not render the FSA's powers to compel evidence useless: they will still be able to use compelled evidence to suggest new lines of inquiry, to justify an injunction or an order for restitution or disgorgement, or to proceed against a person other than the one who gave the evidence.[21]

---

[18]Clifford Chance, Appendix 5; LIBA, Appendix 9, para 10; Lord Steyn, Appendix 3; Lord Lester, Appendix 2, para 15.
[19]Paragraph 229.
[20]CP 17, paragraph 108.
[21]Q 33.

LEGAL ASSISTANCE

21. Secondly, "Subsidised legal assistance will...be made available in appropriate cases to individuals who do not have sufficient means".[22] The Government is considering[23] how this scheme will work, and whether it will be an extension of Legal Aid or a free-standing scheme.

PROTECTION FOR THOSE WHO TAKE "REASONABLE STEPS"

22. "The Government...is considering whether to introduce explicit protections for people who take reasonable steps to make sure that they do not breach the primary provisions [of Part VI]".[24] The Minister explained that the intention is to protect those who operate with proper precautions, with due care and in good faith in areas where the Code of Market Conduct is silent. "Of course we do not want to sanction people for the effects of actions that are unforeseeable".[25]

23. The London Investment Banking Association (LIBA) would prefer the offence itself to include a mental element;[26] and Herbert Smith consider that the FSA should be required to prove intent to abuse the market, rather than merely being able to point to an absence of reasonable steps.[27] However we are satisfied that what the Government now proposes would broadly meet the recommendation in paragraph 270 of our First Report.

CODE AS AN ABSOLUTE SAFE HARBOUR

24. "The Government proposes to make compliance with express provisions in the code [of market conduct] an absolute defence against proceedings for breach of the market abuse provisions."[28] The Minister confirmed that the proposed safe harbour would extend only to compliance with express provisions of the Code, not to actions as to which the Code was silent.[29]

25. This is in line with a view expressed by the FSA towards the end of the first part of our inquiry;[30] but it goes further than we recommended in our First Report.[31] We recommended that "the draft Bill should provide a safe harbour for behaviour that complies with the FSA Code of Market Conduct except where the FSA proves that the person responsible for it intended to engage in market abuse or exhibited recklessness or possibly negligence about the abusive effect of the behaviour". The Minister explained that the Government has been advised that, even if the Bill did so provide, action against someone who had fully complied with express provisions of the Code would be unlikely to succeed.[32]

26. In our First Report we considered the case for extending the safe harbour further, to include conduct in compliance with the rules of an exchange. We were persuaded that this would not be appropriate, and this remains our view.[33]

---

[22]Q 1.
[23]QQ 17-19.
[24]Evidence, p 3, para 16.
[25]QQ 1, 29.
[26]Appendix 9, para 6.
[27]Appendix 4.
[28]Evidence, p 3, para 16.
[29]QQ 1, 26.
[30]First Report, Appendix 5.
[31]Paragraphs 268-270.
[32]Q 28.
[33]But see LIBA, Appendix 9, para 6.

DEFINITION OF MARKET PARTICIPANT

27. "The Government also proposes to clarify in the Bill that the market abuse regime will only apply to market participants."[34] This meets a point made to us by Lord Hobhouse of Woodborough, another of the Law Lords.[35] The Minister explained[36] that the definition will include participants in UK markets who may be physically located overseas, though she acknowledged that in such cases enforcement presents practical difficulties.

DEFINITION OF MARKET ABUSE

28. In our First Report we considered the proposed definition of market abuse in Clause 56 of the draft Bill, and recommended that it should be made more clear.[37] The Government stands by its original draft.[38]   However most of our witnesses remain of the view that Clause 56 requires clarification, despite the Government's other proposals to improve certainty. According to Lord Steyn, "there is a substantial risk that in respect of market abuse the system will be held not to comply with the Convention principle of certainty".[39] Lord Hobhouse put it thus: "So long as the draft for Clause 56 remains in its present form, there will be a serious risk that it will fail in its objective and, far from providing a scheme which will catch the unscrupulous, will provide them with a means of escape which a properly drafted provision would foreclose."[40] LIBA point in particular to "the unclear and subjective tests in the current drafting of Clauses 56(1)(c) and 58(b) and...the lack of clarity about the 'in relation to' tests in Clauses 56(4) and (5)".[41] We would further observe that the expression "true and fair market" is opaque.[42]

29. We acknowledge the Government's dilemma. It seeks a provision sufficiently wide to make evasion difficult, yet sufficiently clear to stand up in court. **We remain concerned that the current draft of Clause 56 lacks the necessary clarity.** Quite apart from any difficulty which this may cause in court, we are concerned that it may cause businesses to err on the side of caution, thereby deterring innovation.

---

[34]Evidence, p 3, para 16.

[35]First Report, Appendix 60.

[36]Q 24.

[37]Paragraphs 260–263.

[38]QQ 3, 25.

[39]Appendix 3.

[40]Appendix 1.

[41]Appendix 9, para 7.

[42]We note that in the context of accountancy the expression "true and fair" has been the subject of considerable elaboration by the profession.

ANNEX

FINANCIAL SERVICES AND MARKETS BILL
REQUIREMENTS APPLICABLE TO AUTHORISED PERSONS, APPROVED PERSONS AND REQUIREMENTS GENERALLY APPLICABLE*

1 : Authorised Persons

Type of Requirement	Enforcement	Tribunal Hearing	Public Announcement of FSA Decision after full process (including any Tribunal Hearing) completed	Evidential Status
FSA Rules general (cl 70) asset identification (cl 73) endorsed codes made by other bodies (cl 74)** price stabilising (cl 75) financial promotion (cl 76) money laundering (cl 77) auditors and actuaries (cl 196) *FSMB refers only to "rules". Term covers rules at high level of generality (which FSA refers to as principles) as well as detailed rules*	FSA enforcement and action under the Bill by other persons (details below) Contravention is not an offence and does not affect validity of transactions (cl 81)	Yes in respect of FSA enforcement action (details below)	Not generally mandatory; will depend on nature of enforcement action taken or FSA policy (details below)	Rule can state that compliance with, or contravention of, it tends to establish compliance with or contravention of another rule (cl 79) Breach of a rule containing this statement is not itself actionable (cl 79)
	FSA public censure (cl 135)	Yes	*Necessarily, yes*	
	FSA financial penalty (cl 136)	Yes	*FSA's general policy will be to announce but it suggests that there may be exceptional cases*	
	FSA withdrawal of authorisation (cl 27)	Yes	*As for fines. Also person may be removed from public register of authorised persons (cl 33)*	
	FSA intervention (not viewed as disciplinary sanction by FSA) (Pt XI)	Yes	*FSA's view is that appropriateness depends on circumstances of case*	
	FSA restitution order (cl 206)	Yes	*No stated policy*	
	FSA can ask court for injunction (cl 202) or restitution order (cl 204)	N/A	*N/A*	

* These tables seek to identify three things: (i) the main types of requirements that apply to authorised persons (sole traders, companies, partnerships and unincorporated associations that are authorised to carry on regulated activities) and approved persons (senior employees of authorised persons or of their contractors) and also certain requirements that are generally applicable; (ii) the consequences of failing to comply with these requirements; and (iii) the status of guidance or codes of conduct that may relate to these requirements. They do not attempt to enumerate every individual provision of the Bill under which a contravention may arise or a sanction may be imposed

** PR, para 5.10 states that the general power for the FSA to endorse codes is to be withdrawn. It is possible that a more restricted power may be included instead

I : Authorised Persons (contd)

Type of Requirement	Enforcement	Tribunal Hearing	Public Announcement of FSA Decision after full process (including any Tribunal Hearing) completed	Evidential Status
	Civil law claim by private persons unless rule excludes this or it is a rule about having/maintaining financial resources (cl 80)	*N/A*	*N/A*	
	Civil law claim by other persons if rule provides for it (cl 80)	*N/A*	*N/A*	
FSA Guidance (cl 87) – it is standing guidance if it is in writing/other legible form and is intended to have continuing effect – guidance (standing or otherwise) may be on any matter	N/A	N/A	N/A	No formal evidential status
FSA Modifications/Waivers (cl 78) FSA can modify/waive its rules (other than asset identification rules) in their application to an authorised person	N/A	N/A	N/A	N/A

II : Approved Persons

Nature of Requirement	Enforcement	Tribunal Hearing	Public Announcement of FSA Decision after full process (including any Tribunal Hearing) completed	Evidential Status
Statement of Principles (cl 48)	FSA enforcement (cl 50) (details below) but no FSMB action by other persons (cl 48)	Generally Yes (details below)	Not generally mandatory; will depend on nature of enforcement action taken or FSA policy (details below)	N/A
	FSA fine (cl 50)	Yes	FSA's general policy will be to disclose but it suggests that there may be exceptional cases; FSA expressly authorised to publish information about any decision not to impose a fine (cl 53)	
	FSA public statement of misconduct (cl 50)	Yes	Necessarily, yes	
	FSA prohibition on employment (cl 40)	Yes	FSA policy as for fines	
	FSA withdrawal of approval (cl 47)	Yes	FSA policy as for fines	
	FSA can ask court for injunction (cl 202) or restitution order (cl 204)	N/A	N/A	
Codes of Practice (cl 48) code must accompany any statement of principles	Non-compliance with code of practice may amount to contravention of statement of principle to which it relates (cl 48)	N/A	N/A	Code may be relied upon so far as it tends to establish whether or not conduct complies with statement of principle (cl 48); has evidential value but is not conclusive
Requirements Applicable to Authorised Persons	Liable to enforcement action if knowingly concerned in contravention by authorised person (cl 50); types of enforcement action as above	Generally Yes (details above)	As above	N/A

III : Requirements Generally Applicable – Market Abuse and Criminal Offences

Type of Requirement	Enforcement	Tribunal Hearing	Public Announcement of FSA Decision after full process (including any Tribunal Hearing) completed	Evidential Status
Market Abuse (cl 56)	FSA can fine any person (cl 58) or can ask the court to fine (cl 64)	Yes for FSA decision to fine	Not mandatory; no stated FSA policy	N/A
	Authorised persons may also be also subject to FSA action (withdrawal of authorisation/intervention) as for contravention of rules (Table I)	Yes (as Table I)	As Table I	N/A
	FSA can ask the court for an injunction (cl 203) or restitution order (cl 205) against any person	N/A	N/A	N/A
	No FSMB action by other persons	N/A	N/A	N/A
	Imposition of fine does not affect validity of transactions (cl 66)	N/A	N/A	N/A
Code of Market Conduct (cl 57)	Helps to determine whether behaviour amounts to market abuse (cl 57)	N/A	N/A	Code may be relied upon so far is it tends to establish whether or not conduct complies with code of market conduct (cl 57); has evidential value but is not conclusive
FSA Guidance (cl 87) *No FSA power to waive or modify market abuse provisions*	N/A	N/A	N/A	No formal evidential status
Criminal Offences eg, misleading statements and conduct offences (cl 212)	FSA can prosecute through the criminal courts	No	N/A	N/A

PROCEEDINGS OF THE COMMITTEE RELATING TO THE REPORT

DIE MARTIS, 2° MARTII 1999

Present:

Lord Burns	Mr Nigel Beard
Lord Eatwell	Mrs Liz Blackman
Lord Fraser of Carmyllie	Mr David Heathcoat-Amory
Lord Montague of Oxford	Mr David Kidney
Lord Poole	Mr Tim Loughton
Lord Taverne	Mr James Plaskitt
	Mr Barry Sheerman

The Orders of Reference are read.

The declarations of relevant interests are made:
Lord Burns (Non-executive Director, Legal & General Group plc)
Lord Eatwell (Director and independent board member, Securities and Futures Authority; adviser, EM Warburg Pincus & Co International Ltd)
Lord Fraser of Carmyllie (Chairman, International Petroleum Exchange; Director, Nova Technology Management Ltd; invited Director, London Metal Exchange)
Mr David Kidney MP (Equity partner in solicitors' practice, Jewels & Kidney, Stafford)
Mr Timothy Loughton MP (Director, Fleming Private Asset Management)
Lord Poole (Chief Executive, Ockham Holdings plc, a holding company with interests in financial services in general and insurance in particular, and director of group of companies; Member of the Stock Exchange; registered insurance broker; formerly Chief Executive of a UK regulated bank and a UK firm of stockbrokers)
Lord Taverne (Non-executive Chairman, OLIM Convertible Trust plc; non-executive Deputy Chairman, Central European Growth Fund plc; non-executive Director, Axa Equity & Law plc; Chairman, Axa Equity & Law Life Assurance Society plc)
Viscount Trenchard (Director, Robert Fleming International Ltd).

It is moved that Lord Burns do take the Chair.—(Mr Barry Sheerman).

The same is agreed to.

(For remaining Minutes of Proceedings relating to the First Report see HL Paper 50-I, HC 328-I, pages 99-109).

DIE MARTIS, 18° MAII 1999

Present:

Lord Eatwell	Mr Nigel Beard
Lord Fraser of Carmyllie	Mrs Liz Blackman
Lord Haskel	Mr David Heathcoat-Amory
Lord Montague of Oxford	Mr David Kidney
Lord Taverne	Mr Tim Loughton
Viscount Trenchard	Mr James Plaskitt

Lord Burns, in the Chair

The Orders of Reference are read.

The Joint Committee deliberate.

Ordered, That the Joint Committee be adjourned to Wednesday 19th May at 3.30 pm.

DIE MERCURII, 19° MAII 1999

Present:

Lord Fraser of Carmyllie
Lord Haskel
Lord Montague of Oxford
Lord Poole
Viscount Trenchard

Mr Nigel Beard
Mrs Liz Blackman
Mr David Heathcoat-Amory
Mr David Kidney
Mr Tim Loughton
Mr Barry Sheerman

Lord Burns, in the Chair

The Order of Adjournment is read.

The proceedings of Tuesday 18th May are read.

The Joint Committee deliberate.

The following witnesses are examined:

Mr Sydney Kentridge, QC
Mr James Eadie

The following witness is further examined:

Ms Patricia Hewitt MP, a Member of the House of Commons, Economic Secretary to the Treasury

Ordered, That the Joint Committee be adjourned to Monday 24th May at 3.30 pm.

DIE LUNAE, 24° MAII 1999

Present:

Lord Haskel
Lord Montague of Oxford
Lord Poole

Mr Nigel Beard
Mrs Liz Blackman
Mr David Heathcoat-Amory
Mr David Kidney
Mr Tim Loughton
Mr James Plaskitt
Mr Barry Sheerman

Lord Burns, in the Chair

The Order of Adjournment is read.

The proceedings of Thursday 19th May are read.

The Joint Committee deliberate.

Ordered, That the Joint Committee be adjourned to Thursday 27th May at 10.30 am.

DIE JOVIS, 27° MAII 1999

Present:

Lord Fraser of Carmyllie	Mr Nigel Beard
Lord Haskel	Mrs Liz Blackman
Lord Poole	Dr Vincent Cable
	Mr David Heathcoat-Amory
	Mr David Kidney
	Mr Tim Loughton
	Mr Barry Sheerman

Lord Burns, in the Chair

The Order of Adjournment is read.

The proceedings of Monday 24th May are read.

The Joint Committee deliberate.

A draft Report is proposed by the Chairman, brought up and read.

Ordered, That the draft Report be read a second time, paragraph by paragraph.

Paragraph 1 is read and agreed to.

Paragraph 2 is read, amended and agreed to.

Paragraph 3 is read and agreed to.

Paragraphs 4 and 5 are read, amended and agreed to.

Paragraphs 6 to 17 are read and agreed to.

Paragraph 18 is read, amended and agreed to.

Paragraphs 19 to 23 are read and agreed to.

Paragraph 24 is read, amended and agreed to.

Paragraphs 25 to 28 are read and agreed to.

Paragraph 29 is read, amended and agreed to.

Resolved, That the Report, as amended, be agreed to.

Ordered, That revised versions of Tables I–III from the First Report be annexed to the Report.

Ordered, That memoranda received by the Committee be appended to the Minutes of Evidence.

Ordered, That the Chairman do make the Report to the House of Lords and Mr Barry Sheerman do make the Report to the House of Commons.

Ordered, That the Joint Committee be adjourned.

LIST OF WITNESSES

Wednesday 19 May 1999

Ms Patricia Hewitt, MP, Economic Secretary to the Treasury, Mr Sydney Kentridge, QC, and Mr James Eadie

LIST OF MEMORANDA INCLUDED IN THE MINUTES OF EVIDENCE

HM Treasury: Parts V, VI and XII of the draft Bill in relation to the European Convention on Human Rights

LIST OF APPENDICES TO THE MINUTES OF EVIDENCE

LIST OF MEMORANDA REPORTED TO THE HOUSE BUT NOT PRINTED

The following Memorandum has been reported to the House, but it has not been printed. A copy has been placed in the House of Commons Library, where it may be inspected by Members. Another copy is in the Record Office, House of Lords, and is available to the public for inspection. Requests for inspection should be addressed to the Record Office, House of Lords, London SW1A 0PW (tel. (0171) 219 3074). Hours of inspection are from 9.30 am to 5.00 pm on Mondays to Fridays.

Justice in Financial Services

MINUTES OF EVIDENCE

TAKEN BEFORE THE JOINT COMMITTEE ON FINANCIAL SERVICES AND MARKETS

WEDNESDAY 19 MAY 1999

Present:

Lord Burns (in the Chair)	Mr Nigel Beard
Lord Fraser of Carmyllie	Mrs Liz Blackman
Lord Haskel	Mr David Heathcoat-Amory
Lord Montague of Oxford	Mr David Kidney
Lord Poole	Mr Tim Loughton
Viscount Trenchard	Mr Barry Sheerman

Memorandum from HM Treasury
Parts V, VI and XII of the Bill in relation to the European Convention on Human Rights

INTRODUCTION

1. The Joint Committee's report of 27 April invited the Government to respond to a number of concerns which have been raised during the Government's consultation and by witnesses to the Joint Committee about the compatibility of the draft Bill with the European Convention on Human Rights (referred to hereafter as the "Convention"). These concerns have centred on the new power for the FSA to fine any market participant, regulated or unregulated, who engages in market abuse. The Government welcomes the opportunity to explain its position and the extension of the period of the Committee's inquiry for this purpose.

THE EUROPEAN CONVENTION ON HUMAN RIGHTS AND THE UK

2. It may be helpful before turning to those concerns to set out some of the general background in this area. The Government is determined to ensure that people's fundamental human rights are recognised and protected by the force of law. The Human Rights Act 1998 gives effect to the Government's manifesto commitment to incorporate the rights and freedoms guaranteed by the Convention into UK law. This Act will fundamentally alter the way in which the courts approach the interpretation of statutory provisions.

3. The courts will be under a duty to interpret legislation in a manner compatible with the Convention rights. Incompatible subordinate legislation may be quashed in certain circumstances or declared incompatible. Primary legislation which cannot be given a meaning compatible with the Convention rights may be formally declared incompatible by a court. Though such a declaration will not affect the validity, continuing operation, or enforcement of the provision, it will trigger a new power allowing a Minister to make a remedial order to amend the legislation to bring it into line with the Convention rights. People who believe that their Convention rights have been breached will be able to rely on those rights in any legal proceedings involving a public authority. The Human Rights Act also contains a specific requirement for the Minster in charge of a Bill to make a statement on the compatibility of the provisions of any new Bill with the Convention rights.

THE NEW REGULATORY REGIME

4. When considering the design of the new regulatory regime, the Government has therefore considered extremely carefully the question of its compatibility with Convention rights. The Government is determined to set up a regulatory system which will provide effective protection for consumers and for the operation of the financial system as a whole. The UK financial services industry is highly successful and vitally important to the UK economy. It accounts for 7 per cent of GDP and employs over one million people. The financial markets support enterprise, helping to provide funds for investment and growth. The source of these funds is the public's savings, which are entrusted to the industry. There is, therefore, a strong and shared interest in having clear, robust, and effective regulation. But the Government is equally concerned to have a system which is fair, and is seen to be fair, and which is fully protective of human rights.

THE CONVENTION AND THE DRAFT BILL

5. In considering the appropriate protections for human rights in the context of the draft Bill, witnesses to the Committee have drawn attention to the requirements of Articles 6 and 7 of the Convention. These Articles draw a distinction between the determination of civil rights or obligations and the determination of criminal charges. It is important to note that a matter which is treated as a civil or administrative proceeding for *domestic* purposes may, nevertheless, be treated as one which involves the determination of criminal charges for *Convention* purposes. What the Convention ensures is that particular, additional, safeguards are available where

what is at issue is the determination of a criminal charge in Convention terms, irrespective of the domestic classification of the proceedings in question.

6.   Article 6(1) of the Convention provides that in the determination of civil rights and obligations everyone is entitled to a fair and public hearing within a reasonable time by an independent and impartial tribunal established by law. The draft Bill provides for this by setting up a fully independent Tribunal to be administered under the auspices of the Lord Chancellor's Department. Any person against whom the FSA proposes to take regulatory action will have the right to have the matter referred to the Tribunal to determine whether action should be taken and, if so, what that action should be. Following consultation on the draft Bill the Government announced that it will be making a number of changes to the Bill to make clearer the precise nature and role of the Tribunal. During the course of the Committee's inquiry, the Government also had a welcome opportunity to clarify to the Committee the interaction of the Tribunal and the FSA's internal arrangements. The Government welcomes the Committee's broad satisfaction with these arrangements and is giving careful consideration to its recommendations.

7.   The right to a fair and public hearing before an independent and impartial tribunal applies equally in the case of a person charged with a criminal offence (in both the domestic and Convention sense). However, the Convention affords such a person certain additional protections over and above those applying in civil cases. In particular the European Court of Human Rights has judged that answers given under compulsion may not be used in criminal proceedings against the person from whom those answers were compelled. As clause 104(5) of the draft Bill indicates, the Government intends that protection should be provided against such use in criminal proceedings under the Bill, for example in respect of insider dealing.

8.   Article 7(1) of the Convention sets out a prohibition on retrospective criminal provision. This has been interpreted as including the principle that an offence must be sufficiently clearly defined in law so that an individual may foresee the legal consequences of his actions.[1]

9.   In considering which Convention protections it would be appropriate to incorporate into the draft Bill the Government looked carefully at the jurisprudence of the European Court of Human Rights. Although the jurisprudence is still developing and may be subject to interpretation, there are a number of factors which are relevant to the characterisation of proceedings as civil or criminal for Convention purposes. The first factor is the characterisation of the proceedings in domestic law, although a civil categorisation in domestic law is not conclusive for Convention purposes.[2] Second, there is the nature of the conduct at which the provisions are directed and, in particular, the overlap with the criminal law. Third, there is the question of whether the measure is directed at the population as a whole, like tax law or road traffic laws, or whether, on the contrary, it is aimed at a particular group of persons possessing a special status the regulation of which is justified to preserve the proper and orderly functioning of the group.[3] Fourth, there is the nature and level of any penalty. The more punitive and severe the penalty, the more likely it is that the proceedings will be characterised as criminal under the Convention.

DISCIPLINE

10.   Although the Government has carefully considered the contrary arguments which have been advanced, it remains firmly of the view that the disciplinary regime applying to authorised firms under Part XII of the draft Bill, and the similar disciplinary powers in respect of approved persons under Part V, would be classified by the Courts as involving the determination of civil rights and obligations for the purposes of the Convention. The scope of the disciplinary regime is limited to a defined set of persons who are part of a regulated community; that is authorised persons and certain of their employees. The requirement for those who choose to undertake financial services business to become part of this regulated group is necessary for the protection of the public. The conduct covered by the regulatory regime is analogous to that which would be covered by regulation of a profession. Although the Financial Services Authority can take disciplinary action where people breach the rules, and these actions can have a deterrent element, they only apply to a subsection of the population and are part of a regime which is essentially protective rather than punitive.

11.   The Government accepts that the nature and size of the potential penalty are also relevant factors under Convention jurisprudence.[4] However, the fact that a fine is imposed does not in itself lead to a conclusion that the proceedings are criminal.[5] Nor does the power to award high financial penalties (which is vital if the

---

[1] *Kokkinakis v Greece* A 260-A (1993) 17 EHRR 397.
[2] *Benham v United Kingdom* (1996) 22 EHHR 293.
[3] *Ozturk v Germany* (1984) 6 EHRR 409; *Ravnsborg v Sweden* (1994) 18 EHRR 38.
[4] *Bendenoun v France* (1994) 18 EHHR 54.
[5] *Brown v United Kingdom* (1998 unreported).
[6] *Brown v United Kingdom* (1998 unreported) and *Air Canada v United Kingdom* (1995) 20 EHRR 150.

objective of protecting the public is to be realised) in itself make the provisions criminal in nature, given their essentially disciplinary character. It is relevant in this context that there is no provision for imprisonment in default of payment of a fine, which is on the contrary recoverable as a civil debt under the draft Bill.[1]

MARKET ABUSE

12. The main purpose of the power to impose a fine for market abuse is also protective. There is no doubt that markets, and the interests of those who deal on them, are damaged if abuse becomes commonplace. The Government welcomes the fact that the Committee accepts in principle the need for a new regime to complement the existing criminal offences. A regime which offers an effective means of combatting abuse serves to protect those who use the markets. The Government recognises, however, that the likely Convention characterisation of the new market abuse regime applying to all market participants is less clear cut than for the disciplinary regime applying only to the regulated community. The same factors are of course relevant. There are two main differences which make the position less certain in respect of the market abuse fining power. First, the market abuse regime is conceptually different from the regulatory regime. It is not concerned with regulating the entry to a regulated community and the conduct and standards of that community. It applies to anyone who participates in the financial markets, a potentially much wider group defined by economic activity rather than by the narrower test of having privileged access to an occupation which is regulated for the protection of the public as a whole. The second difference is the fact that there are significant similarities between the market abuse regime and the criminal offences of insider dealing and market manipulation in terms of scope, content and purpose.

13. The Government's view is that there are reasonable arguments to suggest that the market abuse fining regime would be classed as civil proceedings for Convention purposes. However, having considered the matter further in the light of comments on the draft Bill and the evidence of witnesses to the Committee, notably Lord Lester and Lord Hobhouse, it recognises that there is a real possibility that the market abuse fining power may be classified as criminal for those purposes. That being so, the Government has decided to ensure that additional Convention protections are put in place in the new Bill.

CONSEQUENCES FOR THE DRAFT BILL

14. In order to avoid any risk of a finding that the Bill does not fully comply with the Convention requirements, a change needs to be made to the Bill. This is to ensure that protection against the use of compelled statements is put in place for proceedings to impose a fine for market abuse. Subsidised legal assistance will also have to be made available in appropriate cases to those who do not have sufficient means. The Government will be looking further at how this might be achieved.

15. The Government is satisfied that the Bill provisions for market abuse fully meet the Article 7 requirement for certainty. The European Court of Human Rights has recognised that many laws are inevitably widely drawn.[2] This is particularly so where an area is subject to change. Further interpretation by a Tribunal or higher Court is not an objectionable feature. The Government has, though, taken steps to provide greater certainty by requiring the FSA to produce a code of market conduct which will provide examples of the kinds of behaviours which are acceptable and unacceptable. While the Government understands the desire for certainty in this area, it is of the view that the right approach is to set out the broad mischief on the face of the Bill and rely on the code, which will be subject to full consultation with market participants, to provide more of the detail. To set out greater detail in the Bill would risk leaving loopholes which the unscrupulous could exploit.

16. However, the Government has considered carefully the Committee's recommendation for introducing more certainty by making changes to the status of the code. The Government agrees that there is scope for making helpful changes here. It is important that only abusive behaviour is deterred. The Government therefore is considering whether to introduce explicit protections for people who take reasonable steps to make sure that they do not breach the primary provisions. In addition the Government proposes to make compliance with express provisions in the code an absolute defence against proceedings for breach of the market abuse provisions. The Government also proposes to clarify in the Bill that the market abuse regime will only apply to market participants.

17. The Government believes that with the changes proposed in this memorandum the new market abuse fining regime will be compliant with the Convention.

14 May 1999

---

[1] *Brown v United Kingdom* (1998 unreported) and *Air Canada v United Kingdom* (1995) 20 EHRR 150.
[2] *Muller v Switzerland* (1988) 13 EHRR 212, 226 (paragraph 29); *SW v United Kingdom* (1995) 21 EHRR 363, 399 (para 36).

Examination of Witnesses

Ms PATRICIA HEWITT, a Member of the House, Economic Secretary to the Treasury, MR SYDNEY KENTRIDGE, QC, and MR JAMES EADIE examined.

Chairman

1. Good afternoon, Minister, and welcome to the Joint Committee again. We have seen a lot of people since our last session, which was about two months ago, although sometimes I feel it seems like a lifetime. We are very grateful for your early response to the Committee's suggestion that the Government should respond to the concern that we heard in some of the evidence about the proposed market abuse regime and the whole question of ECHR issues. We have looked at the paper and we have asked some of those who gave evidence earlier to comment on the paper. We have already heard from Lord Hobhouse and Lord Lester and we are hoping to hear from some others by the end of the week. It is then our intention to complete our work by Thursday 27 May and to issue a second report as soon as possible afterwards. We do not expect it to be a long report. Our ambition at this stage is limited to trying to bring together the evidence we receive and to point out where there are substantial measures of agreement and where there are still some differences. I would like to ask whether there is anything by way of opening statement that you would like to make. It might also be of interest to the Committee if there is anything you can say about what your plans might be for responding to the other points in our first report and the progress of the Bill generally.

(Ms Hewitt) Thank you very much indeed, my Lord Chairman. It is a great pleasure to be back with your Committee. Perhaps I could start by introducing counsel whom we have retained to advise the Treasury on this matter: Sydney Kentridge QC and James Eadie. They have very extensive knowledge and experience in this area. I thought it would be very helpful to the Committee if you were able to hear directly from them on matters relating to the European Human Rights Convention jurisprudence and for them generally to help me answer questions so that you are not getting the legal opinion at second hand from me; you are getting it directly. If it would assist the Committee, when I have made some introductory remarks I would like to ask Mr Kentridge also to give some introductory remarks about how they see this area. I would also very much like to welcome the report that you issued from this Committee at the end of April. As you indicated, you have done the most extraordinary amount of work in a very short space of time and I and my colleagues are very grateful to you for that. I must say, if I may, that the report not only contains a number of extremely perceptive and helpful suggestions but it was also a great pleasure to read and I would like to congratulate you on that. It is not always true of parliamentary committee reports. I and my colleagues are now looking very carefully at that report and considering the conclusions and recommendations in it. I will certainly want to respond to each of those conclusions and recommendations. I will do so in due course as we prepare the Bill for introduction. It is obviously not something that I

wanted to rush so I will not be giving you a detailed response to that report in the session this afternoon. I hope that that will be acceptable to the Committee, except for some points that bear directly on the matters that we are considering today. Today of course we are looking directly at the whole issue of the compatibility of the disciplinary and the market abuse regimes with the Convention and the Human Rights Act. As I said when I gave evidence before, we have had the whole issue of compatibility with the Convention at the forefront of our thinking as we have developed and consulted on the detailed proposals in the Bill. As I indicated before, we are determined to certify that the provisions in the Bill are compatible with the Convention and we will do that on introduction. I believe that the Bill is fundamentally sound. I set out the reasons why in the memorandum that I have already let you have, but I think it would be helpful if I just summarise the main points. The objectives that we have in designing this new legislation are, first of all, to ensure that there is effective, proportionate regulation of financial services and, secondly, to ensure that that regulation fully protects people's human rights. As we discussed last time I was here, we all as consumers benefit from strong, cost effective regulation. It makes us more confident in entrusting our savings to the financial services industry and the industry in turn benefits from that confidence. I think it is very important that we are not naive in confronting the need to deal with people who are prepared to profit unfairly in the financial services industry and we need to be alert to the damage that they can do to the great majority of honest individuals and firms and more generally to the financial system and the economy as a whole. We want, and we will get, a regime that is fair but it is not going to be a regime that is soft on people who take unfair advantage of market position or privileged information to abuse the markets. That is why we are giving the FSA an effective range of statutory powers but at the same time we have to ensure that effective regulation does not ride roughshod over human rights. We are determined to ensure that it does not. We do not regard the European Human Rights Convention as an awkward stumbling block that we have to find a way around. We have put it right at the heart of our own legal system by incorporating it through the Human Rights Act. The Convention of course requires through Article 6.1 that in the determination of civil rights and obligations a person has the right to a fair hearing by an impartial tribunal. Article 6 and Article 7, together with the case law, confer further safeguards that are relevant when what is at issue is a criminal offence as characterised in Convention terms. That of course includes the presumption of innocence, the need for a sufficient degree of certainty in legislation and restrictions on the admissibility of compelled evidence. Domestic criminal offences obviously attract all of the Convention criminal protections but sanctions that are

[Chairman *Cont*]

not criminal in our domestic law may nonetheless be criminal for Convention purposes and that is really at the heart of much of what I think we will be discussing this afternoon. If I may turn first to the disciplinary regime, we have no doubts that the disciplinary regime and the provisions that cover employment in regulated activities meet the Convention requirements already. They are not criminal either for domestic or Convention purposes. They are disciplinary regimes that are concerned with protection of consumers and they apply to a regulated community. They are analogous, in other words, to the licensing and disciplinary regimes that concern the conduct, standards and discipline of a profession, including of course the legal profession and the medical profession. That is the disciplinary regime on the one hand. On the other hand, we have the market abuse regime. I think that the classification of the market abuse regime is less clear cut. We still believe that there are good arguments that it be characterised as civil for Convention purposes and that is because it is a protective regime aimed at safeguarding confidence in the major United Kingdom markets. As I think we would all agree, it is vital to sustain confidence in the markets because if they are damaged it impacts ultimately on economic growth in this country and everybody's standard of living. There are two key differences between the fining regime for market abuse and the disciplinary regime. First of all, the market abuse regime extends as it must to market participants who are not members of the regulated community, so it covers everybody who participates in the market for the simple reason that the markets can be and are damaged by abusive behaviour by unregulated persons. The *Sumitomo* case is a very good example in point. The world copper markets were distorted for years because of abusive trading by the unregulated head of copper trading in that firm. That is one key difference. The other key difference is that in the case of the market abuse regime there are significant similarities between the regime and the criminal offences that already exist of insider dealing and market manipulation. The new regime is distinct from the criminal offences and we have made it quite clear that where there is criminal behaviour it will be prosecuted through the criminal courts where the evidential and public interest tests are met, but nonetheless that overlap does colour the nature of the market abuse fining regime to some extent. Those two differences do not mean in our view that the market abuse fining regime will necessarily be characterised as criminal under the Convention. That will be a matter for the courts. I do accept that there is a degree of uncertainty there and as a result we have decided to introduce the additional criminal Convention protections in this regime. What we need to do, as I indicated in the memorandum, is to change the Bill to restrict the use of compelled statements that have been obtained during an FSA investigation in proceedings to impose a market abuse fine on the person who gave that compelled evidence. In other words, we need to Saunders-proof the market abuse fining regime. Subsidised legal assistance will also have to be made available in appropriate cases to individuals who do not have sufficient means. The Government will be looking further at how that might be achieved. There are three other changes to the regime that we do intend to make and I would like to mention them, although they are not in fact necessary for Convention purposes. The first one that we have touched on before is that we will clarify in the Bill that the market abuse regime only applies to market participants. That was always the intention, but I think there was some concern about how it had been given effect. Secondly, we will make compliance with the express provisions of the code on market abuse a complete defence against a charge of market abuse. If the behaviour in question was not referred to in the code, then of course the FSA will still be able to take action if they consider the conduct to be abusive. No code can cover every possible eventuality that arises over the years to come. Finally, we will be looking at ways to ensure that people who take proper precautions to ensure that they do not breach the primary legislation cannot then be fined for market abuse. We want people to act with due care when they are interacting with the financial markets, but of course we do not want to sanction people for the effects of actions that are unforeseeable. The regime is designed to protect the efficiency of markets. It is designed to deter unacceptable behaviour, not acceptable behaviour, and clearly there needs to be a reasonable degree of certainty in achieving that. If it would be convenient, my Lord Chairman, perhaps I could hand over to Mr Kentridge now to make some further remarks on the Convention jurisprudence in this area.

2. Of course.

(Mr Kentridge) My Lord Chairman, we are grateful to you and to the Members of your Committee for giving us this chance to address you. If I may briefly introduce myself, I am a practising barrister in London. I have some experience of human rights cases in various different contexts. I did represent HMG in the *Saunders* case in Europe and I should say at once unsuccessfully. My friend Mr James Eadie was with me in that case. He has an unrivalled knowledge of the jurisprudence of the European Court of Human Rights and the Commission as it was. He must have appeared in more than 50 cases. If there is any question which arises about any particular decision of the European Court of Human Rights, there is no one better qualified to answer your questions on that. I know that you have had legal views expressed to you by various people and it is not surprising—in fact, even in a clearer context it would not be surprising—that the views of lawyers differ but in the context of the application of the Convention to a new regulatory regime we are all to a certain extent groping. None of us can say with certainty how the courts are going to interpret the Convention in the time to come. We must get what guidance we can from the decisions of the European Court of Human Rights, but it is only guidance. We must remember that when the Human Rights Act comes fully into force these matters will be dealt with in the first place, and one rather hopes for the most part, by the courts of England and of Scotland. In approaching this Convention, they will of course apply the basic principles of our own jurisprudence. The

[Chairman *Cont*]

particular matter on which we have sought to give advice relates to the distinction for Convention purposes between the disciplinary regime on the one hand and the market abuse regime on the other. If I can deal first with the disciplinary aspect of it, we have expressed the view, not dogmatically but with a degree of certainty, that in European Convention terms the disciplinary regime would be characterised as civil and not criminal. We say that for a number of reasons. One is that the objective of the disciplinary regime is to establish and maintain standards of conduct amongst a professional community, not only in the interests of that community itself but in the interests of the public, particularly the investing public, to give them the protection of having their affairs handled by persons of competence and integrity. From a more technical point of view, what characterises this regime as disciplinary and therefore civil rather than criminal is that although disciplinary proceedings might lead to a fine, first, in our own law under this Act it will be characterised as civil and not criminal. That of course is not conclusive in European terms. What is of the utmost importance is that this regime does not apply to the public at large to whom a criminal regime would apply, but it applies only to members of a particular profession or occupation—that is to say, persons or companies who are authorised. In terms of the European jurisprudence, that is a vital point. Thirdly, one looks at the nature of the conduct which is dealt with. The nature of the conduct dealt with is fundamentally not breach of the criminal law but breach of the rules of a particular profession and occupation. Finally, there is the question of what the sanctions are for breach of the rules. The sanctions here could be a reprimand or a suspension or, in a serious case, even a striking off but, in some circumstances, a fine. As I understand the opinion of Lord Lester—and I must say his opinions are always entitled to the highest respect—the matter that worries him is that there may be a fine for an infraction of disciplinary rules. That is so and the reason is that there will be infractions of disciplinary rules which may not be so serious that one will strike off the person concerned or even suspend him from carrying on his occupation but which nonetheless require some sanction and that is where the fines come in. I know that, my Lord Chairman, you and the Members of the Committee have been told that a fine in its very nature is punitive. That cannot be denied. It is, but there is no disciplinary——

Mr Sheerman

3. Do you mean it is not an unlimited fine? I understood it was the unlimited nature of the fine.

(Mr Kentridge) I will assume that it is unlimited and I will try to explain why. The first point I want to make is that the European Court naturally recognises that there are some sorts of proceedings which are disciplinary and civil and not criminal, notwithstanding that there is a fine. The reason I would suggest is a very simple one. The reason is that a disciplinary provision would have no teeth at all unless there were some sanction for infraction. One must realise that very often a fine is the more merciful

sanction. What about the vexed question of the unlimited nature of the fine? Those concerned with drafting this legislation I know have thought very seriously about that. There were only two alternatives. One is a limited fine and the other is an unlimited fine. In that regard, one has to bear in mind the community that we are dealing with. These people in this community are very big players. In the case of some of them and some of the transactions which they undertake, the sort of fine that would bankrupt most people and most businesses may just be the tiniest blip on their balance sheets. I think it is a case where the fine must fit the infraction and the person or company responsible. If one has perhaps an employee on a salary who has broken disciplinary rules, one would assume that the fine would be a moderate fine, but if one had, for example, a case of a deliberate disciplinary infraction by an enormous company anything other than a very large fine would have no effect at all. One must assume—not merely hope—that the Financial Services Authority and eventually the tribunal which will hear disciplinary offences will approach this matter in a reasonable way. They will not make it their business to impose fines which are going to make it impossible for people to live in the community. The other reason, apart from the general principle, which makes us more confident in expressing this opinion is one of the latest cases in the European Court of Human Rights and that is the case of *Brown*. Brown was a solicitor who committed breaches of the solicitors' disciplinary rules and he was fined £10,000. In the circumstances of his case, £10,000 was a very substantial fine. He went to the European Court of Human Rights saying, "But I did not have the protections of the criminal law and proceeding". The Court found that the proceedings were civil on the grounds I have mentioned. They were intended to be civil. The criminal prosecution authorities did not come into it. Failure to pay the fine did not result in going to prison. The rules applied only to the community of solicitors who had subjected themselves to those rules and the fine in the circumstances was regarded as reasonable. One does not want to be dogmatic, but those whom we advise presumably want our opinions and not merely our doubts. This is what I would like to say more generally about the problems with which you are faced here. When it came to the market abuse regime, as the Minister has said, there are very good arguments that that too is civil, but none of us could give a confident opinion on that and therefore, out of an abundance of caution the drafting of this Bill will proceed on the assumption that it will be found to be criminal. Therefore, additional safeguards will be put in, particularly the Saunders safeguard. That is the main safeguard. We believe that with what we have called in shorthand the Saunders safeguard that the market abuse regime will be a safe regime. We have also expressed the opinion, on which we could expand if required, that given the nature of market abuse the general definition of it in Section 56 is adequate from the point of view of the European Convention on Human Rights. If I could conclude on something very general, my Lord Chairman, the Human Rights Act

[Mr Sheerman *Cont]*

which will come into force next year is a practical measure and it has the enormous advantage that these matters of the interpretation of the statutes of this country measured against the European Convention will, for the first time, be matters for English and Scottish courts. I cannot over emphasise the importance of that. One of the real drawbacks of the previous regime was that when a case from this country went to the European Court it had before it no judgment of the English or Scottish courts on the point before it. What will happen now is that the courts of this country, the Court of Session, the Court of Appeal and the House of Lords, will have considered all these points before they go to Europe. I must say that I am confident that a court in this country, looking at the disciplinary regime with its vast experience of disciplinary regimes in this country, will hold that this is civil. One has to take a view on it. This is the view which we have taken and which we have expressed. If one wants to take a negative view of these matters, one has to accept that there is going to be no statute so tightly drawn that some barrister is not going to stand up in court somewhere and say that his client's human rights have been contravened. That just has to be faced and one has to trust the courts of this country to deal with it. May I in conclusion just read to you something which was said by Lord Woolf in dealing with the new Bill of Rights in Hong Kong? What he said, in my respectful submission, applies equally to our new Human Rights Act. He said, "The issues involving this Bill of Rights should be approached with realism and good sense and kept in proportion. If this is not done, the Bill will become a source of injustice rather than justice and it will be debased in the eyes of the public." I have no doubt the courts of this country will approach the Human Rights Act in that spirit. Thank you.

Chairman: Thank you very much for those introductory remarks which I think are very helpful. We heard a lot of points of view during the period when we were taking evidence and we have been very anxious to hear the Government's response to them. We would like to probe a little on some of these issues, first of all on discipline generally and then market abuse and there are one or two questions about overlap.

Lord Fraser of Carmyllie

4. Minister, you are holding an opinion which is clearly less equivocal on discipline than might be traditional. You express some confidence in saying you are firmly of the view. In paragraph ten, you conclude by saying that one of the characteristics of this which leads your counsel presumably to that view is that this applies only to a subsection of the population and is part of a regime which is essentially protective rather than punitive. In the event, some financial services practitioner in the future may be fined personally hundreds of thousands of pounds. He might not only be suspended; he might be deprived of practising as a financial adviser for the rest of his life and he might suffer very serious adverse publicity for all that. Does that not have a punitive quality to it and is it not intended to have a punitive quality? Is it not

perfectly reasonable that it should have a punitive quality to it?

(Ms Hewitt) I think Mr Kentridge has already elaborated on the reasons for our confidence that this is in fact a civil regime. The distinction between protective and punitive is not an absolute one. In the circumstances you describe, clearly the individual would feel that these were pretty punitive sanctions, but the central point here is that the disciplinary regime applies to the limited group of people who have chosen to become authorised persons within the regulatory regime of financial services. The central purpose of the regime is to protect the clients of those authorised persons, just as the purpose of the disciplinary regime for doctors is to protect doctors' patients, or the disciplinary regime for solicitors has as its purpose to protect solicitors' or other lawyers' clients. That protective function is extremely important, but the crucial issue when it comes to the question of characterisation for Convention purposes is that the disciplinary regime only applies to this limited group of people and that it is part of the licensing system, if you like, that the individual who chooses—nobody is forcing him—to become an authorised person within the financial services industry submits himself to when he joins that profession. It is precisely analogous to the other disciplinary regimes and clearly those are civil for Convention purposes just as we believe this is.

5. I am not allowed properly by law to drive my car and drink. It is not primarily for my own purposes; it is for the protection of other people, is it not? To a common law practitioner, the clear distinction that is drawn between what is civil and what is criminal is one that is readily enough understood. I wonder if your legal counsel are confident that there is not prospectively a sort of continuum here. If you start with a rap on the wrist, a small fine to someone, that will be treated as civil but at some indeterminate point, as the activity gets more serious, the fine gets greater and the penalty, the suspension, gets greater. That is likely to be treated by the European Court as criminal and accordingly the difficulty is to determine what characteristics you should give to the proceedings to ensure, as it crosses over that point, that you do have an adequate set of protections in place.

(Ms Hewitt) I think it is confusing that we have one distinction between civil and criminal within our own domestic law that I think we all understand, which is not the same as the distinction between civil and criminal regimes under the Convention.

(Mr Kentridge) That is the sort of question to which one says, "That is a very good question" while trying to think of the answer, but if I may respectfully agree with Lord Fraser I think it is a continuum. That means that one has to make up one's mind where on the continuum one is. My own view is that, even where under a disciplinary proceedings you may have large fines, all the other aspects of it—the fact that unlike the driver under the influence of drink, which is to protect the public and which applies to everyone—this applies only to people who have chosen to become authorised, who have submitted themselves to a disciplinary regime, just as I have submitted myself to a disciplinary regime by becoming a barrister. If you

[Lord Fraser of Carmyllie *Cont*]

consider that aspect of it, I would say one is able to say that this disciplinary part is on the right end of the continuum. Market abuse? You are in the middle. To be cautious you say, "Let us regard it as criminal". I did have a note here through the kindness of Mr Eadie. There have been numerous cases of disciplinary tribunals, not all from this country but which have come before the European Court, where the sanctions include expulsion from your profession which can be much worse than a fine. If I could just give you the names—we have the cases if anyone wants to look at them—in the case of *Guchez v Belgium* it was applied in a case of the disciplinary tribunal over architects, civil. *König v Germany*, doctors, civil. *De Moor v Belgium*, advocates, also civil. Here we have had cases arising from disciplinary proceedings by IMRO which are characterised as civil, although it dealt with the question of whether someone could be in this profession at all. Another very interesting case is *Wickramsinghe*. Those were disciplinary proceedings against a doctor who was struck off the roll. The interesting thing about it is that he was struck off for conduct which was by any judgment criminal conduct, namely the indecent assault of a patient, but in spite of that the European Court of Human Rights said no, this is civil. It disciplines him in his own profession and it is a profession which he has joined, so all of European jurisprudence on disciplinary matters which I am aware of comes down on the civil side of the continuum. I know that there is a French judgment to which Lord Lester has referred you but that raises a different question.

Chairman

6. I think we understand quite clearly this distinction about people who are part of a regulated community. Our question is directed to the last sentence of paragraph ten which slightly puzzled us because you make the point that it only applies to a subsection of the population, but then you go on to say, "... and are part of a regime which is essentially protective rather than punitive." In the latter part of that sentence, we do not quite understand the distinction between "protective" and "punitive" because it seems to us that, by the very nature of some of the arguments you were making about very deep pockets in some of these firms, there must be a punitive element here. It would appear that you are bringing into account here two sets of arguments, and yet whenever we raise the second one you simply return to the first one.

(Ms Hewitt) In a sense, we were simply elaborating on the first argument. Clearly, that distinction is not a hard and fast one and, yes, there does need to be a punitive or, if you like, a deterrent element within the disciplinary regime, but it is the nature of the disciplinary regime that makes it clearly civil.

Mrs Blackman

7. It is the use of that punitive element and the degree of that punitive element in that argument that is quite difficult to square.

(Ms Hewitt) This comes back to two points that Mr Kentridge has made. The first one is that the fining powers of the regulator in the disciplinary regime have to be capable of being proportionate both to the mischief that is being caught and the size of the player. It can be perfectly proper to have a limit on the fines that you might impose on GPs or even on lawyers, although some of them are quite wealthy, but when you are looking at authorised persons that include legal persons, that include companies, within the financial services industry, you are talking here about companies that are capitalised for billions of pounds. Therefore, either you simply do not put a limit on the fine that can be imposed or you put a limit that is so high that it is meaningless in terms of any effective restriction on the FSA. The issue is simply that when the FSA or indeed the independent tribunal come to decide, within the disciplinary regime, on a fine then of course it has to be proportionate both to the mischief and to the player, the person concerned, but it is the size of some of these players that means there should not be a limit. Equally, my second point is that it is of the essence of a disciplinary regime, a regime that licenses entry into a continued participation within a profession, within a set of activities, that the regulator has to be able to suspend or indeed to expel somebody from that profession. Of course, deprivation of livelihood is an immensely serious sanction and one that clearly will have and is intended to have a deterrent effect. That does not change the nature of the disciplinary regime from being civil.

Lord Montague of Oxford

8. I was very relieved to hear your use of the phrase that disciplinary policy should not be soft. I think that was the word you used. In view of the situation as you have described it, I wonder whether it would be helpful or desirable if the FSA had a transparent fining policy. It might be very difficult but it might also be helpful and necessary.

(Ms Hewitt) I think that is something that the FSA can certainly consider. I cannot recall—forgive me—whether it is something that you raised with Mr Davies when he was here before.

9. No.

(Ms Hewitt) It is certainly something that they might want to consider and which I think could have the beneficial effect of making the disciplinary regime even more transparent and spelling out in a sense consequences of actions. My first reaction would be that it is not desirable for the FSA to tie itself down to a kind of tariff because it is essential both that the enforcement committee of the FSA and the tribunal itself should be able to look at all the circumstances of the case, the nature of the mischief, the impact that it has had and the nature of the player. I do not think you can capture that in a tariff scale: "If you do this it will be £10,000" and, "If you do this it will be a million." You simply could not do that.

10. And also to maintain public confidence that it is working effectively.

(Ms Hewitt) I am reminded that under clause 59, which I had forgotten, the FSA has to prepare and

[Lord Montague of Oxford *Cont*]

publish a statement of its policy on fines, but I certainly do believe that that policy needs to be about the general principles and the criteria that will guide those decisions, rather than a kind of tariff scale from which you read off the amount of the fine.

Lord Poole

11. Could I ask your advice on a small point of information? On the continent, when people join the sorts of occupations that are regulated that lead to the view that the disciplinary procedures are civil, do they in any sense, in signing up, give up their rights to being treated as criminals? You were citing doctors and architects. I wondered whether there was anything to be said for somebody who becomes a member of such an occupation saying, "Am I to understand that these are civil proceedings that I am signing up to?".

(Mr Kentridge) I certainly do not know enough about what happens in other countries. Certainly when you join an occupation or profession in this country you do not explicitly give up anything. If my Lord Chairman would allow me to add something to that, what one must always bear in mind—we have been stressing the difference between civil and criminal—the fundamental difference we have been discussing is whether compelled statements can be used against you. What one must remember is that, by common law, what everyone is entitled to, whether he has joined a profession or not, is fundamental fairness. Whatever you call the regime, even if it is civil, you have to be treated fairly. If there is a case against you, you have to be told what it is. You have to have a chance to answer it. Unfair evidence cannot be used against you, even if your own statements can be, but not if you have been tricked or trapped into giving them. One must remember the distinction here is not between an unfair civil regime and a fair criminal regime; it must be fundamental fairness in both cases with a little extra protection in the criminal one.

(Mr Eadie) In some of those cases that Mr Kentridge mentioned, the dispute in Strasbourg was not between civil and criminal. It was whether those people in those professions had any civil rights at all. The argument that was at the centre of those cases was whether or not, because it was effectively administrative or within a closed profession, they could even claim the protection of paragraph one of Article 6 by saying, "We have a civil right". That is even one stage below, if you like, the distinction which we are arguing about, which is between civil on the one hand and criminal on the other.

Mr Sheerman

12. Nearly all the examples you and Mr Kentridge have given are professions regulated by themselves. Because they are professions, they are regulated by a long term body of rules, well acknowledged and used. I am not saying that working in the City is not a profession but they certainly do not operate in the same way as lawyers, doctors or architects. What we are seeing is that the Financial Services Authority is imposing discipline, not a group of peers deciding on the rules of the relevant society. It is true that you have

only been using that sort of comparison, is it not? Is it not different?

(Mr Kentridge) I will ask Mr Eadie. The IMRO cases?

(Ms Hewitt) While you think about that, I would stress that if you look, for instance, at the medical profession and the powers of the General Medical Council, although you are right that it is peers of doctors who are deciding it, the powers come from the Medical Act 1983 and originally from an Act of 1858. They are not self-regulatory bodies. Of course there will be quite substantial peer involvement in the processes we are setting up under the Financial Services Act.

(Mr Eadie) IMRO, at the time of the *APB* decision, which is the one Mr Kentridge referred to, was a self-regulatory organisation. It was contract based as opposed to statute based.

13. Can I switch track a little here? That was really on the back of Lord Poole's question but when Mr Kentridge made his remarks he mentioned a French case. I think he was referring to the *Oury* case which does seem to throw a rather different light on the penalties. I can see Mr Eadie smiling but it is in the Lester response. This has been a very interesting Committee, almost like a university seminar. When Lord Lester came back on his second bite, he did mention this *Oury* case which raises different questions. Perhaps you could respond to that.

(Ms Hewitt) We have all enjoyed reading the *Oury* decision sometimes in French and then more helpfully in English. Let me just stress that of course decisions of the French courts do not decide the characterisation of any part of our Bill and future Act for Convention purposes.

(Mr Kentridge) I have read a translation of the *Oury* case. Like most French judgments, it is very succinct. I will not say "opaque". It is not all that easy to understand but there are certain aspects about it. Firstly, although they said there that the presumption of innocence had to apply as it would in a criminal case, I do not know that they characterised the matter as criminal, but whether they did or not if you read the facts of that case, what happened was that the managing director of a company apparently was charged with deliberately putting out false information about the company into the market. As I read that, that is more equivalent to our market abuse regime than to disciplinary. In fact, I did see a note from Lord Lester and he speaks of it as a regulatory provision, not a disciplinary provision. I would read it as a case about a regulatory provision closer to the market abuse side of the continuum. That is why I do not read it myself as an authority that the disciplinary provision would be criminal. On this case, if this case had come before an English court or a Scottish court, without any reference to the European Convention, the appeal would have been upheld. One of the people who was sitting as a judge had, outside court before the hearing, made a statement to the effect that they were guilty. It was a case like the Queen in Alice in Wonderland: sentence first, verdict afterwards. It was a most shocking case. I do not think you would find anything there that says that a disciplinary hearing is criminal.

Viscount Trenchard

14. I would like to ask Mr Kentridge to go a little bit further on this question of whether or not a presumption of innocence should be afforded to those charged with offences under the disciplinary regime. It seems to me that the punishment may, in certain circumstances, be disproportionately large. If you work in the City and even if you have committed some breach which may have been unintentional, because there is also the question of the absence of intent, the punishment may be so great it may not only include a fine but your name may be in the newspaper so you will probably lose your job and you are probably unemployable by any other firm for the rest of your career. Yet, if the regime is civil, you do not benefit, as I understand it, from a presumption of innocence.

(Mr Kentridge) If I could just make a distinction, as I understand it, there will certainly be a presumption of innocence. There will never be a case under a disciplinary regime where the disciplinary body can simply say, "Here is the charge against you. Prove that you are innocent." The presumption of innocence has a number of aspects. The presumption of innocence, in general terms, will be there but there is one aspect, and one aspect only, of it which will not. One aspect, and only one, of the presumption of innocence in a criminal case is that if you have been compelled to give testimony and have not given it voluntarily it cannot be used against you. As I understand the thinking behind the statute, it has been thought that it is perfectly legitimate and not against fundamental fairness in a disciplinary regime to be able to use against someone his own answers. If I could again go to my profession, if the Bar Council were to say, "We have had a complaint against you and you have to answer it because if you do not that is a disciplinary offence in itself. What did you do? What do you say about that?", I would have to answer, but I would not find anything extraordinary in the fact that, when I am charged, my own account and explanation is there before the tribunal. After all, supposing I had said, "Yes, I am guilty and I have no excuse". The thinking is that it would be quite extraordinary in a disciplinary proceeding, as distinct from a criminal one, that that cannot be put before the tribunal. It is not a case of no presumption of innocence and a presumption of guilt. The real distinction we have been discussing, as I understand it, is simply whether that one particular protection is appropriate in a disciplinary context and the thinking in the statute is that, in a purely disciplinary context, there is no need for that protection and in fact it might stultify all the disciplinary proceedings. I think in law it is a very real distinction but, as I understand it, that is the policy behind the distinction.

(Ms Hewitt) The presumption of innocence applies in both regimes, disciplinary and market abuse.

Chairman: I think this is a convenient moment to move on to the issues of market abuse and criminal justice.

Mr Beard

15. Before we leave that Chairman, could I just make one point? Whereas Mr Kentridge has been very clear in saying that the regime for disciplinary cases is civil irrespective of the size of the penalty, we have an opinion from Lord Lester and Miss Monica Carss-Frisk that gives an equally firm view in the opposite direction. I quote: "It may be criminal for the purposes of Article 6 of the ECHR where the nature of the offence or the nature and degree of severity of the penalty is so indicated." That is quite the opposite and I just wondered if you would like to comment and explain how that sort of difference could arise?

(Ms Hewitt) I have here two lawyers who agree but you can generally find two who disagree.

(Mr Kentridge) I have great respect for what Lord Lester says but I believe that the *Brown* case in the European court supports my view and I do not believe that the *Oury* case in France really supports Lord Lester's view. But in the end, Mr Beard, whatever the differences one does have to take a view. No-one can give a guarantee that his view is right but we have considered it and this is the view which we have come to, for the reasons which I have tried to state. I do not know that I could really say more, my Lord.

16. Thank you. Could I go back to the question of compelled evidence because it has been made clear that there will be provision made to avoid compelled evidence being used in a prosecution which is criminal. There was an article in *The Financial Times* on 15 May which implied that compelled evidence would be avoided in virtually all proceedings. Could you confirm the appropriate interpretation?

(Ms Hewitt) No, the memorandum sets out the correct position. The Saunders-proofing restrictions on the use of compelled statements in proceedings to impose a market abuse fine do not apply to proceedings that are disciplinary, even if they lead to a fine.

Mr Loughton

17. Minister, in paragraph 14 of your memorandum on the subject of legal aid, you were considering subsidised legal assistance in appropriate circumstances. What are those appropriate circumstances and how do you envisage it is going to be paid for?

(Ms Hewitt) This is a matter, Mr Loughton, which we are still considering. The Convention requires legal assistance to be made available where that is necessary in the interests of justice. I think what that suggests is clearly one has to look at the means of the person, the individual or the company, against whom market abuse fining proceedings are being brought. One also has to look at the complexity of the case and whether or not it is actually reasonable to expect the individual concerned to put his own case or whether legal representation is going to be required in order for that person to have a fair hearing. There might well be other considerations but, as I indicated in my opening statement, we are looking at how that provision of the Convention can best be given effect to.

[**Mr Loughton** *Cont*]

18. I think "in the interests of justice" is a pretty wide phrase and I am thinking of cases which have been touted here recently where compliance officers have been prosecuted and have been ditched by their former firms and effectively left on their own. How would you envisage the means-testing of whether it is in the interests of justice for an individual, as opposed to the former firm, who, of course, can afford to pay large bills, and also there is the point about how we are going to pay for this?

(Ms Hewitt) We have not yet decided what kind of subsidised legal assistance we wish to put in place for market abuse fining cases, whether it should be an extension of legal aid or whether there should be a self-standing scheme that simply applies to proceedings under this Act. So that is something that we are having a look at and I have not got a scheme that I can offer you at the moment. Clearly we also have to look at how any such scheme should be paid for but the situation you describe is precisely the kind of situation I think we do need to take account of because if you have proceedings against a large company then it is perfectly reasonable for you to expect the company to be able to pay for representation. If you have proceedings against somebody who is extremely wealthy, then the same thing probably applies, but if you do have proceedings against someone who, although those proceedings have not been concluded, has nonetheless been dismissed from his firm and does not have substantial accumulated wealth, then I think you probably need to take a different view, and that is what we are looking at in order that we can come forward with an appropriate scheme for subsidised legal assistance.

19. Are you ruling out a levy on firms?

(Ms Hewitt) I have not ruled anything out yet. I have not made a decision on this issue.

Lord Montague of Oxford

20. Whilst you are having a look at this, will you be looking at the same issue in relation to the ombudsman scheme?

(Ms Hewitt) The ombudsman scheme is a very different matter, Lord Montague, because, of course, the whole purpose of the ombudsman scheme is to provide for a fairly informal and fast, albeit fair, system for resolving disputes generally between clients and firms. So I am not sure that the same considerations do, in fact, arise there, but certainly the ombudsman scheme must be fair and thereby meet Convention standards.

Lord Haskel

21. Minister, you said in your introductory remarks that you propose to make it clear in the Bill that the market abuse regime will apply only to market participants. May I press you and ask you how you intend to define who a market participant is?

(Ms Hewitt) I am not the parliamentary draftsman, happily, and he will wish to come forward with suggestions for the precise form of words. I am certainly not going to try and do the drafting this

afternoon in front of the Committee, but I think the point that has been made to us is that the words in the Bill at the moment might be misinterpreted to include people who are very clearly not market participants. They might, for instance, in an example given to me at the London Metal Exchange, be warehousemen in a copper warehouse in Africa who have gone on strike. Their strike might indeed have some very serious consequences upon the market but quite clearly they are not market participants and it is in no sense our intention to catch them. So we do need, I think, to look at how we can more precisely give effect to our intentions there because what we are looking at really are people who are buying or selling or holding investments that are covered by the markets that are embraced by the new regime.

22. But there is going to be a very grey area of people who maybe are amateurs but who still participate in the market. You have day traders in the United States. Would they be market participants or not? This is going to be very difficult.

(Ms Hewitt) Clearly if you have people who are buying or selling stocks, perhaps on the Internet, they are market participants and, indeed, there are a number of stories now emerging from the United States of America about people using the Internet in order to achieve a false, entirely artificial, rise in the price of their stocks, false information put out on the Internet in order to raise the price of perhaps some Internet-type stock in order that somebody can cash it in and then, of course, when the untruth of the information is discovered, the price falls back. They have become quite common; they are known as "pump and dump" ploys. So there are amateur, but not necessarily naive, participants who quite clearly should be caught by a market abuse regime.

Lord Fraser of Carmyllie

23. But is it still your desire, is it still your objective, to catch Mr Hamonaka if he has never left Japan but has nevertheless significantly distorted the London market?

(Ms Hewitt) Yes, and Sumitomo was, of course, fined substantial fines by the American regulators for that particular scam, that market abuse. The British regulators were powerless because at that point, and this is the situation now, you have criminal offences, narrow class of behaviour, wide class of persons; you have the disciplinary regime, broader class of behaviour, narrower class of persons, but you did not have what the market abuse regime will provide under this Bill, which is the broader category of behaviour and the broader group of market participants, and I think you need that, just as they have that in the States.

24. I am aware of what Sumitomo did. Your summary is absolutely correct. The Minister has been traditionally British not to exercise extraterritoriality. I just want to be clear that you do believe that it is important to achieve a degree of extraterritoriality through this device, do you?

(Ms Hewitt) We do have global financial markets and clearly behaviour by someone who may be physically thousands of miles away can have a very

[Lord Fraser of Carmyllie *Cont]*

damaging effect upon the markets here. They are global markets. There are certainly practical difficulties where you are trying to catch people, particularly individuals who are thousands of miles away but we do not think that is a reason for narrowing the scope of the Bill.

Chairman: Could we move on to the issue of certainty.

Mr Heathcoat-Amory

25. Market confidence and, indeed, the requirement of justice clearly require certainty and this is a requirement of the Convention on Human Rights. You say in your memorandum that the Government is satisfied that the Bill's provisions for market abuse fully meet the Article 7 requirement for certainty. I note here that you say that the Bill itself meets this requirement, so you are not relying on some subsequent regulations or code of conduct or whatever, but when I look at the Bill, and in particular existing clause 56, I find something that is anything but certain. It is highly subjective and it relies on the supposed attitudes of other market participants to the release or non-release of some information. Moreover, it does not actually criminalise anything, it only authorises elsewhere in the Bill the FSA to fine that person if, in their opinion, it constitutes market abuse. So I think this is anything but clear if it is to constitute criminal law, which you now say it is. Do you intend, therefore, to redraft or alter this section of the Bill, and if that is so, when could you do it because obviously there is otherwise a gap between your intentions and what is, in fact, the case?

(Ms Hewitt) Thank you, that is an extremely interesting and also rather comprehensive question. The first point is that when you say we accept that this is criminal, I do just want to stress we are not talking about a domestic criminal regime like the normal criminal law. That is not what the market abuse regime is. As Mr Kentridge has indicated, you can argue both ways, whether or not even under the Convention a market abuse regime is civil or criminal, but we think it is as well to be ultra-cautious here and put in those extra protections. On the matter of certainty, we believe that the provisions of the Bill do, in fact, meet the Article 7 requirements for certainty. That refers both to the actual words on the face of the Bill but also the requirement on the FSA to produce a code of conduct on market abuse. The European Human Rights Court has recognised in several cases that many laws are inevitably widely drawn, and I think that is particularly so when you are dealing with areas that are changing very rapidly, and there is no doubt financial services move very fast indeed. So we have a reasonably general set of provisions within the Bill itself. Those are then supplemented by the requirements for a code of market conduct and, of course, the FSA is consulting at the moment on a draft. That code can never be completely comprehensive. It is quite impossible to anticipate fully everything that market participants might get up to in the years to come, but we think that the code will provide a very valuable additional degree of certainty beyond what would be provided if we simply relied on the Bill and

then on the development of case-law. I have to say that was the approach that was taken in the United States of America. You had basic mischiefs that had not been elaborated upon in any great detail by the Securities and Exchange Commission but there has been a build-up of case-law over 50 years. We think we can get greater certainty and faster certainty by using the code of conduct. Of course, we are also saying, as I explain in the memorandum, that compliance with the express provisions of the code must be an absolute defence to a charge of market abuse and I think, taken together, that gives probably the highest degree of certainty that we can achieve certainly a reasonable degree of certainty and one which I believe is fully compliant with the Convention. Mr Kentridge, do you want to add to that answer?

(Mr Kentridge) I do not really think so, Mr Heathcoat-Amory. The fact is that the European Court of Human Rights has said on many occasions that some sorts of even true criminal offences can only be stated in general terms. The more you define it, it has sometimes been said, the more loopholes there are. But I am not a draftsman either. I believe that the tribunal and the court would make sense of that definition.

(Mr Eadie) One final thing perhaps. They have also accepted in Strasbourg that it is acceptable under Article 7, which is the nub of the Convention concern here, for relatively broadly expressed laws to be developed by case law, and that applies both to the development of broadly framed statutory provisions and, indeed, to the common law itself, the classic example being the case of marital rape which went recently to Strasbourg. The strong complaint being made by the rapist was: "I did not realise at the time I committed the rape that it was an offence to rape your wife," and there was genuinely, surprisingly perhaps, some doubt under the common law as to whether that was the position at the date the offence was committed. Strasbourg takes the view it is acceptable for laws of that kind to be developed on a case-by-case basis. So they do not exclude judicial interpretation and, indeed, development of legislative provisions.

Viscount Trenchard

26. Minister, could I continue a little bit on the same topic. As far as the code is concerned, I think we were very pleased that the Government set such importance by it and that it will be subject to full consultation with market participants, and also, as you have explained, that you propose to make compliance with its express provisions an absolute defence against proceedings. So that, on the one hand, would seem to provide a much greater degree of clarity, but then what worries me is that it seems to me that even though conduct might not be prohibited by the code, it might still be found to be in breach of the statutory precepts in clause 56. I worry how that situation might sit with the Convention.

(Ms Hewitt) I think, as you suggest, Lord Trenchard, we partly touched on that in the immediately preceding question, the code of conduct is very important because it can spell out specific mischiefs that do constitute market abuse and it can also spell out, if you like, positive courses of action

[Viscount Trenchard *Cont*]

that would mean somebody was not engaging in market abuse, and I think that is essential, but it would be impossible for any code to deal with every possible eventuality or to anticipate everything that people might do in future. Therefore, I think the FSA must be able, in the years to come, to proceed against people for market abuse, as defined in clause 56, where the actions that have given rise to the market abuse are not referred to in the code itself, where it is silent, because otherwise we will have a situation where somebody will think of something, a mischievous person will think of something that is absolutely an abuse of the markets but somehow, because it has not been dealt with in the code, the FSA will not be able to proceed and that will be clearly an unacceptable state of affairs.

27. I worry about that, particularly because subsection (9) explains that behaviour includes inaction as well as action, so I find that conceptually quite difficult.

(Ms Hewitt) The inaction could arise, for instance, where, in order for somebody to deal fairly on the markets, they have to supply full information to the markets. It might be information about something that is changing within a company, and if they do not provide that information, so inaction, depending what else is going on, that could constitute market abuse. It may be a situation that constitutes an abusive squeeze, where simply holding on, refusing to close off a position or to make certain supplies available, is an integral part of the abusive squeeze and thus the market abuse. It is an inaction rather than a positive action but it is nonetheless integral to the behaviour that constitutes market abuse and the FSA must be able to deal with that.

Mr Kidney

28. Minister, we were interested that you said that the code will provide an absolute safe harbour for those who comply with its positive provisions, whereas in our report we thought a qualified safe harbour depending on a person's intentions in what they actually were doing when they complied with the strict letter of the code. Why have you been more generous than we would have been?

(Ms Hewitt) We have looked at this very carefully here and we are very mindful of the desire in the industry for as much certainty as possible as well as the requirement of the Convention for appropriate certainty, and we felt it was right here to say that if somebody has complied with the express provisions, then really they should not be vulnerable to an action against them by the FSA. Indeed, I have to say that even if we had gone for a more qualified position, I think it is very unlikely that the tribunal or the courts would have upheld action by the FSA in that circumstance.

29. Where the code is silent you said that they would not be seeking punishment of people who take reasonable steps to comply with the spirit of the code. What do you have in mind by "reasonable steps"?

(Ms Hewitt) We are looking at the kind of draft provision which will take into account the situation of people who act with due care and in good faith and

the code may be silent on the matter. Someone who acts with due care and in good faith should not really be proceeded against for market abuse, but we are looking at the appropriate draft provisions in this area.

30. Would you expect the FSA to issue guidance from time to time explaining the kinds of things they would think reasonable, and if so, would then the guidance be some kind of safe harbour, just as the code is?

(Ms Hewitt) I think one has to draw a distinction here between guidance and the code. I have no doubt at all that the FSA will want to update the code from time to time, but obviously when it does so it will go through the appropriate consultation before it finalises any changes to the code. The question of guidance is a rather different one and we are certainly not persuaded that guidance from the FSA, which could be to a specific authorised person or firm, should have the same weight as the code. In any case, I do not think that is a matter that needs to be dealt with on the face of the Bill itself.

Chairman: Could we move on, finally, to the whole question of overlapping regimes. We have some general questions about how we now work in a world where we seem to have two approaches.

Mrs Blackman

31. If an authorised person engages in market abuse, then necessarily they will have broken the FSA's general rules. Does that present a dilemma in terms of the distinction you make between the two regimes, the disciplinary regime and the market abuse regime?

(Ms Hewitt) No, I do not think it does present a dilemma. In practice, when it comes to market abuse by authorised persons you actually have three regimes. You have the criminal regime, because it may be that the authorised person should actually be prosecuted for insider trading or whatever; you have the market abuse regime, which applies to authorised persons but also to non-authorised participants, and then you have the disciplinary regime. In that situation the FSA, I think, will, first of all, have to decide whether or not a criminal offence has been committed, and if so, whether or not a criminal prosecution will be appropriate, but if a criminal offence and a criminal prosecution are not in question, then they will need to look at the possibility of taking action under the market abuse regime, and if they do so and if they compel that individual to answer questions, then, of course, they will not be able to use the answers that have been compelled in proceedings for a fine. Then they have the question of disciplinary proceedings. Now it may well be the case that an authorised person who has committed market abuse and perhaps been fined for that market abuse under the market abuse regime is also, in the view of the FSA, no longer a fit and proper person to be authorised for participation in the financial services industry, in which case it is perfectly proper for the FSA to proceed against that person under the disciplinary regime. What they cannot do is fine the authorised person under the market abuse regime and then come back for a second

[**Mrs Blackman** *Cont*]

bite of the cherry, a second fine, under the disciplinary regime, but they certainly can proceed under the disciplinary regime for a suspension or a complete ban on that person's participation in the markets. Precisely the same thing happens in the legal profession and in the medical profession. Indeed, Mr Kentridge gave the example of the doctor who was struck off for conduct that, on the face of it, constituted a criminal offence of indecent assault. I think in that case the victim did not want to prosecute. There were no criminal proceedings but it was totally proper for the General Medical Council to proceed via disciplinary proceedings and strike the doctor off.

32. Do you think the Bill makes those distinctions clear enough?

(Ms Hewitt) It will.

Lord Fraser of Carmyllie

33. May I ask one practical question about this, Minister? If to Strasbourg-proof the actions of the FSA you make attendant upon almost everything they investigate, everything they do, and take all those steps that ensure you would not fine someone in breach, like no longer relying on compelled statements, do you think the disciplinary side of things is actually workable or are they actually just going to clog up?

(Ms Hewitt) I do not think that taking proper steps, as we are doing, to ensure that we comply with the Convention on Human Rights Act is going to make the regime unworkable at all. First of all, in the market abuse regime where the Saunders-proofing will apply, the FSA will still be able to compel people to answer questions. They will not be able to use the compelled evidence against the individual who gave those answers if they are seeking to fine them for market abuse, but they will be able to use the evidence that they compelled in restitution and injunction cases, civil proceedings. They will also be able to use the information they obtain to suggest other lines of enquiry or to get documentary evidence that will then be available to them, and, of course, the evidence that is compelled from one person can also be used against somebody else in proceedings for market abuse. On the disciplinary side, the issue is not whether Saunders-proofing would make the disciplinary regime unworkable. The issue is simply that Saunders-proofing is not justifiable and that comes back to the issue we were talking about earlier about the nature of a disciplinary regime and the licensing of people who choose to participate in a profession or some other authorised activity. From a policy point of view I see no reason whatsoever why financial traders and other authorised people should be treated any differently from doctors or lawyers.

Mr Sheerman

34. May I say, Minister, that much of what I have heard this afternoon has set my mind at rest, these questions of whether this is clearly compatible with the new European Court of Human Rights obligations that we have decided to sign up to. But I have been pushing right through this Committee's proceedings, whenever possible, to get international comparisons. On the one hand, I do think that in regulation matters, whatever industry you are in, whether it is in the environmental sector or any other, many people do not like making comparisons across regulatory regimes or cross-national comparisons. Is there anything we can learn from people who have signed up to the European Court on Human Rights that have similar regulatory regimes? What is their practice? They have been involved with that for some years, although from what you and your two colleagues here today have been saying, my mind has been put at rest. That is a real level of achievement. My mind is at rest in a sense, because we must in ECHR go through the English courts first. We are going to build up the system gradually of what has been the real experience over a number of years in comparable countries to our own?

(Ms Hewitt) I think your general point about the need to learn from the regulatory regimes in other countries is absolutely right and we also, in developing this Bill and the policy behind it, looked to financial services regulation in other countries as well as in our own country and tried to learn from the good as well as the bad. When it comes to the specific matter of the Human Rights Convention, I think you have to recognise that the jurisprudence is developing very fast and, therefore, rather than looking at how does the French or the Italian or whatever regulatory system deal with the Convention, the best thing is for us to get the best possible and the most up-to-date legal advice on the matter and then make a judgment about how we should proceed. As we have seen in the *Oury* case for whatever reason they clearly had not anticipated that those proceedings were going to be found wanting, although, as Mr Kentridge has outlined, even without the Convention they would have been found wanting under our conception of natural justice. When it comes to hearings in front of our British courts on Human Rights Act issues, I am sure that they will also want to look at cases that have been settled in other parts of the European Human Rights Convention area but, indeed, they will probably want to look elsewhere as well, because, of course, in Canada and Australia, for instance, they have had Human Rights Acts for much longer and there is a developing body of jurisprudence there that can also be brought to bear on the interpretation of the Act, but that is not specific to financial services.

35. But are there any countries where there has been real difficulty in running a regulatory regime like this because of the constant problems of running into these sorts of legal difficulties with the courts?

(Ms Hewitt) Not that I am aware of.

(Mr Kentridge) I have really not been into it at all. I just cannot answer that.

Lord Montague of Oxford

36. May I enquire whether there is a country which has an ombudsman scheme where we can learn

[Lord Montague of Oxford *Cont]*

whether hearings are necessary and what effect that might have on the operation of the existing ombudsman scheme, which, of course, is at the moment relatively informal?

(Ms Hewitt) There is, of course, Sweden, from which the father, the parent, of the ombudsman scheme came, but, as I indicated earlier, the scheme will have to provide for a fair and public hearing in order to comply with the Convention and the FSA are aware obviously of the need for compliance and we will expect the operator of the ombudsman scheme to make rules for such a hearing. But I think the important thing is not to undermine the essential nature of the ombudsman scheme to provide for, as I said, relatively informal, non-legal proceedings so that we can get disputes resolved.

Chairman

37. Minister, I think we must let you go. We said we would try and finish shortly after five. We are very grateful for the evidence you have given, and your colleagues. I think it has been very helpful. As you know, throughout this our aim has been to try to clarify people's positions and to try and get views to move as close as possible towards each other. I hope we have taken another step in that direction. We will see how some of the other people from whom we have asked for written evidence respond to it, but I hope that we are continuing to shuffle towards something which has maybe a wider degree of agreement than when we started this process.

(Ms Hewitt) Thank you very much indeed and I shall look forward very much to the Committee's next report.

APPENDICES TO THE MINUTES OF EVIDENCE

TAKEN BEFORE THE JOINT COMMITTEE ON FINANCIAL SERVICES AND MARKETS

APPENDIX 1

Memorandum from The Right Honourable The Lord Hobhouse of Woodborough

Thank you for sending me a copy of the Treasury Memorandum dated 14 May and inviting me to comment upon it.

The Memorandum is specifically directed to the impact of the European Convention on Human Rights upon the present draft of the proposed Financial Services and Markets Bill. As the question whether a bill in accordance with the draft is compatible with the Convention would be a justiciable issue, I must continue to decline to express an opinion. But the Memorandum also touches upon questions upon which I have given evidence and I will shortly respond to these.

The Memorandum recognises the distinction between the disciplinary parts of the draft Bill and the provisions of Part VI. However the mere fact that both are designed to be protective does not provide a relevant similarity. The important point is that the disciplinary provisions apply to the regulated community whereas the market abuse provisions apply to the world at large. Paragraph 12 of the Memorandum repeats that Part VI applies to "anyone who participates in the financial markets". As I have said in my evidence, the present draft does not so provide.

Paragraph 15 of the Memorandum refers to the question whether clause 56 is sufficiently certain for the purposes of the Convention. I express no view about this. But it is a mistake to believe that there is no need to address the drafting of clause 56. The existing draft is defective in ways to which I and other witnesses have drawn attention independently of the Convention. These defects of drafting can be remedied if the Treasury so chooses. So long as the draft for clause 56 remains in its present form, there will be a serious risk that it will fail in its objective and, far from providing a scheme which will catch the unscrupulous, will provide them with a means of escape which a properly drafted provision would foreclose.

17 May 1999

APPENDIX 2

Memorandum from Lord Lester of Herne Hill QC

1. I am grateful to the Chairman of the Joint Committee on Financial Services and Markets for the opportunity to give the Committee my views on HM Treasury's Memorandum, confining myself to the concerns about the compatibility of the draft Bill with Article 6 of the European Convention on Human Rights.

2. The Treasury's Memorandum contains several welcome developments in the Government's thinking, in the light of the Joint Committee's First Report. These developments make it more likely that the eventual legislation will stand up to legal challenge on human rights grounds.

3. However, there remain important respects in which the draft Bill, read with the Treasury's memorandum, remains vulnerable to successful legal challenge for breaches of Convention rights, with continuing and avoidable legal uncertainty.

4. I agree with the general summary of the requirements of Articles 6 and 7 of the Convention, contained in paragraphs 5 to 9 of the Treasury's memorandum.

5. The Government's decision (paragraph 13) to treat the market abuse fining power as criminal in nature, for the purposes of the safeguards in Article 6 of the Convention, and to introduce additional Convention protections in the Bill is welcome. So too is the decision (paragraph 16) to make compliance with express provisions in the code an absolute defence against proceedings for breach of the market abuse provisions, and to clarify in the Bill that the market abuse regime will only apply to market participants.

6. If the Government decides (paragraph 16) to introduce explicit protections for people who take reasonable steps to make sure that they do not breach the primary provisions, this will further reduce the risk of a successful legal challenge.

7. According to a report in the *Financial Times,* on 15–16 May, the Government also proposes to exclude the use of compelled evidence from civil proceedings that could lead to a fine. This is not mentioned in the Treasury's memorandum, but, if it is correct, it will again serve to reduce any mismatch between the Convention and the legislation, giving effect to the Joint Committee's recommendation (Report, paragraph 205).

8. Unfortunately, the Government remains of the view (paragraph 10) that the entire disciplinary regime applying to authorised firms under Part XII of the draft Bill, and the similar disciplinary powers in respect of approved persons under Part V, would be classified by the Courts as involving the determination of civil rights and obligations, and not of criminal charges, for the purposes of Article 6 of the Convention.

9. In my view, this is too sweeping an approach, and leaves scope for considerable legal uncertainty and a real risk of a successful legal challenge in a particular case.

10. It is true, as the Memorandum points out, that the scope of the disciplinary regime is limited to a defined set of persons who are part of a regulated community; that is, authorised persons and certain of their employees. I also accept that the requirement for those who choose to undertake financial services business to become part of the regulated group is necessary for the protection of the public, and that the conduct covered by the regulatory regime is analogous to that which would be covered by regulation of a profession. And I accept that most aspects of the regime would properly be regarded as essentially protective rather than punitive.

11. However, these factors are not conclusive. I would respectfully refer the Joint Committee to the analysis in paragraphs 10 to 19 of the Joint Note of Advice of 7 April, given by me and my colleague, Monica Carss-Frisk (Joint Committee's First Report, at pp. 96–98),[1] which has not, in my view, been dealt with satisfactorily in the Treasury's memorandum.

12. The nub of the problem is that, while many disciplinary offences are likely to be classified as civil in nature, some serious disciplinary offences are likely to be classified by the courts as criminal, whether because they effectively cover misconduct which is criminal (e.g., market abuse offences) or because of the risk of the infliction of drastic fines with a dominantly punitive, rather than compensatory or restitutionary purpose.

13. The risk of successful legal challenge is illustrated by the recent decisions of the French courts applying Article 6 safeguards to proceedings for the imposition of administrative fines in the context of financial regulation. The Commission des Opérations de Bourse ("COB") is an administrative authority established to ensure the protection of investors' savings, disclosure to investors, and the proper functioning of the financial markets. The COB is empowered to impose administrative sanctions in respect of breaches of its regulations. The French Cour d'Appel and Cour de Cassation have treated[2] the sanctions as criminal in nature (and hence protected by the presumption of innocence) because of their high level and the publicity attached to them, and the fact that the sanctions are aimed, as in criminal cases, at punishing those who breach the general standards laid down in the COB's regulations, and to deter others from similar misconduct.

14. I am not clear as to how the Government regard this case law and its potential bearing upon the interpretation of the draft Bill.

15. In my view, a careful distinction needs to be made in the Bill between those disciplinary offences which ought properly to be regarded as civil and those which ought properly to be regarded as criminal, so as to ensure that, where appropriate, the FSA respects the presumption of innocence in disciplinary proceedings which it decides to bring.

16. The Treasury's Memorandum has not yet responded to the Joint Committee's recommendation (Report, paragraph 141) that the Government should publish its response on my concern that the proposed immunity for the FSA from suit for damages for acts done in good faith in discharge of its functions may breach the right of access to courts guaranteed by Article 6. In the light of the recent case law of the European Court of Human Rights in several cases against the United Kingdom, I continue to remain concerned about this.

18 May 1999

APPENDIX 3

Memorandum from The Right Honourable The Lord Steyn

By letter dated Friday, 14 May the Secretary of the Joint Committee on Financial Services and Markets wrote to me in the following terms:

> "Lord Burns, the Committee's Chairman, invites you to consider the memorandum and to give the Committee your views, preferably in the form of brief written submission suitable for publication, to reach me by Friday, 21 May. The essential question is, whether in your view the Treasury's memorandum makes it more likely that the eventual legislation will stand up to legal challenge on human rights grounds."

---

[1] As regards our reference (paragraph 19) to Dame Shirley Porter's case, in decision of the Court of Appeal of 30 April, they effectively treated "wilful misconduct", within the meaning of section 20 of the Local Government Finance Act 1982, as criminal in substance, while rejecting submissions that the presumption of innocence (guaranteed by Article 6(2)) had been breached in her case.
[2] See e.g., the *Oury* decisions.

I received a copy of the First Report and, at my request, certain additional information on Monday, 17 May. I received the Bill on Tuesday, 18 May. Given the need to respond by Friday, 21 May, and my involvement every day this week in sittings of the Appellate Committee, time for consideration of this important matter has been extremely limited. Nevertheless, I would like to help so far as I am able to do so.

I respond in my capacity as a judge. In doing so I am expressing provisional views on proposed law reform the effectiveness of which will no doubt be tested in the courts after the Human Rights Act 1998 comes into force. I may have to revise such provisional views in the light of arguments in a concrete case. I write this letter on the understanding that my response will be a matter of public record.

Except for one point, I do not propose to comment on the principles the courts will have to apply after the Human Rights Act 1998 comes into force. It is important to bear in mind that a basic theme of the jurisprudence of the European Court of Human Rights is to find a fair balance between conflicting values and interests. That is how an English court will probably approach the matter when the Human Rights Act comes into force. It is likely to take as a starting point that the new regulatory system must be just and must protect Convention rights, but also to accept as a basis premise that in order to serve the interests of the public it must be effective. In my view the courts are therefore likely to accept the importance of the objective as it is described in paragraph 4 of the Treasury Memorandum dated 14 May 1999. But it may be useful to spell out the twin objectives in the long title to the Bill.

The only specific comments that I am able to make on the somewhat fluid and developing shape of the proposed legislation are as follows:

1. INDEPENDENT TRIBUNAL

It is of vital importance that the precise nature and role of the Tribunal, and the insulation of Tribunal from the FSA's internal procedures, should be clearly spelt out in the legislation. This is an indispensable requirement for the effectiveness of the new system. Paragraph 6 of the Memorandum suggests that the necessary changes will be made. This is reassuring.

2. DISCIPLINE: PARTS V AND XII OF THE BILL

It is an important question whether the disciplinary system is likely to be classified in Convention terms as criminal proceedings. While I recognise the force of the contrary arguments (and notably the point about the potential size of fine) my present view is that it is likely that the courts will generally speaking treat the disciplinary system as involving civil proceedings. But where the disciplinary matters closely overlap serious species of market abuse I regard the position as entirely open.

3. MARKET ABUSE: PART VI OF THE BILL

For reasons given by Lord Lester of Herne Hill it is probable that the courts will classify the market abuse provisions as criminal proceedings. I am glad to see that the Government has decided to ensure that additional Convention procedures are put in place in the new Bill. I have not seen those changes nor any changes designed to deal with Lord Hobhouse's comments in his recent letter on the flaws in clause 56. At present it is apparently intended that the proposed system will continue to be underpinned by a vaguely worded Code, such as is contained in the document headed Part 2: Draft Code of Market Conduct (dated June 1998). In these circumstances there is a substantial risk that in respect of market abuse the system will be held not to comply with the Convention principle of certainty.

My answer to the question put to me is that the Treasury's Memorandum represents considerable progress. But there is clearly much work to be done.

20 May 1999

APPENDIX 4

Memorandum from Herbert Smith

INTRODUCTION

1. Herbert Smith are pleased that both the Joint Committee and the Treasury recognise the importance of addressing the European Convention on Human Rights ("the Convention") issues relating to the Bill. As we have previously indicated, it is essential that this is done. It would be very damaging to the FSA and to the London Markets were there to be a successful Convention challenge to the main aspects of the new legislation.

MARKET ABUSE

2. We are pleased that the Treasury agrees that the market abuse regime is criminal rather than civil for Convention purposes. We therefore agree that Clause 104(5) of the draft Bill should be amended to cover market abuse proceedings as well as criminal ones.

3. We do not consider that the provisions in the Bill defining market abuse fully meet the Article 7 requirement for certainty and consider that a clearer statutory definition should be given. This is also the view of the Joint Committee, see paragraph 263 of the Joint Committee's First Report.

4. In Paragraph 16 the Treasury states that the Government is considering whether to introduce explicit protections for people who take reasonable steps to make sure that they do not breach the primary provisions. The concept of taking reasonable steps not to breach something which is not clearly defined but which is worded very generally is a very difficult one. We look forward to receiving further clarification on what is meant. In the meantime, our view remains that the relevant test should involve showing an intent to abuse.

Paragraph 16 goes on to say that the Government proposes to clarify the Bill in that the market abuse regime will only apply to market participants. In our view it is right to exclude from the regime manufacturers, suppliers and physical users of commodities and there may be other classes who should be excluded. We look forward to clarification on this and, in particular, how "market participants" is defined.

DISCIPLINE

5. There are genuine concerns that the proposed disciplinary regime would be categorised as criminal for Convention purposes. We note that the Government may be proposing to exclude the use of compelled evidence from civil proceedings that could lead to a fine, see paragraph 7 of the Memorandum from Lord Lester of Herne Hill. It is not yet clear whether what is being proposed would involve bringing disciplinary proceedings within Clause 104(5) of the Bill. No doubt this will be clarified.

STATUTORY IMMUNITY

6. In our evidence to the Joint Committee we expressed the view that granting statutory immunity to the FSA would be in beach of the Convention, see Osman-v-UK [1998]. We share the concerns expressed by Lord Lester in his Memorandum at paragraph 16 and hope that this will be addressed by the Government.

21 May 1999

APPENDIX 5

Memorandum from Clifford Chance

Thank you for your letter of 18 May 1999 enclosing the Treasury memorandum and Lord Lester's comments on it, and inviting our views. We have also seen an advance draft of LIBA's comments on the memorandum.

We agree with the observations of both Lord Lester and LIBA and resist the temptation to repeat their points here. The key issue in our opinion is whether it is worth the risk that the FSA disciplinary regime will be challenged, potentially successfully, at some time in the future in the context of a particular case on the grounds that one or more rights under the ECHR were violated because those particular proceedings fell to be characterised as criminal rather than civil for the purposes of the Convention. The Committee may not be in a position to judge now between the competing legal arguments; but it can be fairly certain that such a challenge will be made one day. Therefore, in our view, it ought to express an opinion as to the wisdom of running the risk of paralysis while such challenge is mounted, and disarray if it is successful.

The following points occur to us to be relevant (and in the interests of brevity they do not purport to be exhaustive):

— Undoubtedly the punitive and deterrent use of fines in the disciplinary regimes involves severe penalties by any standard: the Treasury memorandum acknowledges this at paragraph 11.

— The conceptual muddle caused by the introduction of significant fines for punitive and deterrent purposes, introducing what are seen as classically criminal law concepts into a regulatory and therefore civil/administrative law regime, predates the draft Bill. But the process of scrutiny involved in moving from a primarily contractual system to a wholly statutory system has necessarily highlighted the confusion. The Human Rights Act 1998 has sharpened the focus of this process of scrutiny.

— The distinction traditionally drawn between the protective and punitive purposes may ultimately prove in this context to be one without merit. The Treasury's reliance on *"the power to award high financial penalties"* as being *"vital if the objective of protecting the public is to be realised"* illustrates they overlap in any event. Similarly, the use of the powers of public censure, which can cause as much damage to a business as a fine, or to exclude persons from the industry, which deprives a firm or person from pursuing their chosen livelihood, while traditionally seen as regulating a profession for the protection of the public, can be equally punitive when viewed from the perspective of the persons affected and act as a deterrent to others. In this regard we refer to Lord Lester's opinion that *"The decisive test is what is at stake for the individual or firm, the gravity of the offence, and the severity of the potential sanction"* (Joint Note at paragraph 15(c) reproduced in Annex C on page 98 of the First Report).

— Given what is at stake, both for the individual firms and persons involved in any case, and for the confidence of the industry (including its contribution to the economy: see paragraph 4 of the Treasury memorandum), is a minimalist approach to the application of the ECHR appropriate? At the very least, many of the particular disciplinary cases involve alleged offences of such gravity, high stakes for the individual or firm, and potential sanctions of such severity, that as a matter of fundamental fairness (irrespective of the requirements of Convention law), the additional Convention protections should be applied.

— The restrictions on FSA powers when applying the additional Convention protections are not such as to debilitate the FSA in the exercise of its enforcement function. The fruits of compulsorily obtained evidence can be used to build the prosecution case; only the transcripts of compulsory interviews of the person charged are inadmissible as against *that* individual. The civil standard of proof on the sliding scale is unlikely to be materially different in application from the criminal standard in such cases. While in some complex cases financial assistance may be required to ensure equality of arms, such cost alone cannot be a sound reason for denying the other protections.

There is therefore a real risk of the disciplinary regime being held to be criminal for ECHR purposes, with all the consequences that flow from that. We would therefore urge the Committee to recommend to the Government that it should not seek to describe the entire disciplinary regime as civil; that a line should be drawn between the sort of conduct which should attract the safeguards provided by the ECHR; and that that line should be cautiously drawn, so as to ensure that only minor infractions are characterised as civil for ECHR purposes.

21 May 1999

APPENDIX 6

Further Memorandum from Clifford Chance

THE ROLE OF FSA GUIDANCE IN THE NEW REGIME

SUMMARY

The draft Bill empowers the Financial Services Authority (FSA) to issue guidance on the operation of the Act and of any rules made under it as well as certain related matters. However, that guidance has no special status on which market participants can rely.

The FSA will not be the only prosecutor of offences under the new Act. Contraventions may also render contracts unenforceable and give rise to other civil liabilities.

The Bill should treat compliance with FSA guidance on the statutory offences as rebuttable evidence that an accused has established prescribed defences to a prosecution or claims to set aside contracts. For example, it should tend to establish that a person exercised reasonable care to avoid the contravention or that a person reasonably believed that he was not contravening the requirements of the Act.

In contrast, a market participant should be able to place clear reliance on the FSA's guidance on its own rules, codes of conduct, etc., and on the operation of the market abuse provisions. However "unlikely" in practice, the FSA should not be able to give guidance on how to comply with its own rules or the market abuse regime and then take enforcement action against someone who complies with that guidance. In addition, firms that have complied with FSA guidance should not be exposed to claims by private investors that they have contravened conduct of business rules.

The Bill should, however, only give the proposed special status to published guidance. This minimises the risk of any distortion of competition and the disappointment of legitimate third party expectations.

The FSA should not be compelled to issue guidance on request. However, the FSA should be willing to issue published guidance in individual cases as a means of developing policy and responding to particular situations.

We propose specific statutory drafting to implement this proposal.

1. *FSA guidance under the draft Bill*

1.1 The draft Bill empowers the FSA to issue guidance on the operation of the Act and of any rules made under it as well as certain related matters.[1] However, that guidance has no special status on which market participants can rely.

1.2 The Government has stated that it is unnecessary to give a particular status to FSA guidance "because it is unlikely that the FSA would wish to or could properly discipline firms who have been following its guidance".[2]

1.3 However, the FSA is likely to find it necessary to give guidance on the perimeter and other offences prescribed in the new Act. For example, the Government has stated that it expects that "the role of FSA guidance [on the scope of the authorisation offence] will play a significant part in reducing the number of unnecessary authorisations."[3] But the FSA will not be the only prosecutor of offences under the new Act.[4] Contravention of prohibitions in the new Act may also render contracts unenforceable and give rise to other civil liabilities.[5] In addition, contraventions of the FSA's own rules may in some circumstances give rise to civil liability to third parties.[6] It is unjust that the draft Bill provides no recognition of a market participant's compliance with the guidance of the regulator responsible for the administration of the statutory regime.

1.4 Even where the FSA is responsible for enforcement, market participants may take little comfort from the assertion that it is "unlikely" that the FSA would take enforcement action against a firm that has complied with its guidance. Many of the requirements that will be imposed by the new Act and that are likely to be imposed by the rules, codes of conduct, etc., will be very broadly drawn.[7] Firms and individuals face unlimited fines and other significant sanctions for non-compliance. The Bill should explicitly state that, at least in some circumstances, market participants can place reliance on what the FSA has said as to how they can comply with these requirements.

1.5 In addition to securing fair treatment for market participants, giving the FSA's guidance special status under the new Act would enhance the role of guidance as a flexible means of developing the regulatory regime. In its present form, the draft Bill encourages market participants to call for amendments to statutory provisions, secondary legislation and the FSA's rules, codes, etc., to deal with grey areas. If guidance had some special status, it could be used to provide some level of comfort in difficult cases. More comprehensive amendments could then be made at a later stage through statutory instruments or changes to rules, etc. in the light of more complete practical experience.

1.6 However, there are clear policy distinctions between the role that guidance could play in relation to the perimeter and other offences prescribed by the legislation and the role that guidance can play in relation to the FSA's own rules, codes of conduct, etc., and the other matters on which the FSA is empowered to take enforcement action. We discuss these separately below.

2. *Guidance on the perimeter and other offences*

2.1 A number of the proposed statutory prohibitions will provide the accused with a defence to a prosecution where he can show that he has taken reasonable care to avoid committing the offence or that he believed on reasonable grounds that he was not contravening the relevant prohibition.[8] Similarly, the court will, in some cases, be given the discretion to allow the enforcement of an otherwise unenforceable agreement where it is satisfied that the person in question reasonably believed that the transaction was lawful[9].

2.2 The Bill should treat compliance with FSA guidance on the statutory provisions as rebuttable evidence that these defences have been established. The court would not be bound by the FSA guidance. It would be free to reach its own decision on the facts. However, the court should be required to give special weight to the fact that a person has complied with the FSA's guidance. Otherwise, that guidance may be of no more value than the opinion of any other commentator.

---

[1] Clause 87 of the draft Bill. References to clauses are to clauses of the draft Bill.

[2] Paragraph 5.8 of HM Treasury Progress Report on the Financial Services and Markets Bill (March 1999).

[3] Paragraph 1.3 of HM Treasury Consultation Document on Regulated Activities under the Financial Services and Markets Bill (February 1999).

[4] See clause 215. The other principal prosecutors are the Secretary of State and the Director of Public Prosecutions.

[5] See e.g., clauses 14 and 15 (in relation to the authorisation offence), clause 19 (in relation to financial promotion) and also clause 55 (in relation to the employment of prohibited persons and employment of persons without approval).

[6] See e.g., clause 80 (in relation to suits by private persons).

[7] The obvious examples are the market abuse regime (clause 56) and the proposed FSA Principles for Business (see FSA Consultation Paper 13).

[8] See e.g., clauses 12(3) and 13(3) in relation to the authorisation and holding out offence and paragraph 6(2) of Schedule 4 in relation to the exercise of Treaty rights by EU firms (defence if accused shows that he took all reasonable precautions and exercised all due diligence to avoid the contravention); clause 17(4) in relation to financial promotion (defence if accused shows that he believed on reasonable grounds that the communication was lawful or that he exercised all due diligence to avoid the contravention); clause 212(4)(a) in relation to the market manipulation offence (defence if accused shows that he believed on reasonable grounds that conduct would not create false market).

[9] See clause 16(4)(b) and (c) in relation to the agreements made where the authorisation offence has been committed. No similar power is currently granted in relation to agreements rendered unenforceable as a result of a contravention of the financial promotion regime (see clause 19), although our submission to HM Treasury on the draft Bill argues that there ought to be such a provision.

3. *Guidance on FSA rules, etc.*

3.1   In contrast, a market participant should be able to place clear reliance on the FSA's guidance on its own rules, codes of conduct, etc. However "unlikely" in practice, the FSA should not be able to give guidance on how to comply with its own rules and then take enforcement action against someone who complies with that guidance. Also, a firm that has complied with FSA guidance should not be exposed to claims by private investors alleging non-compliance with conduct of business rules or other similar requirements under the new Act.

3.2   Similarly, the FSA should not be able to give guidance on the operation of the vague and unbounded provisions of the market abuse regime and then take enforcement action against a market participant who complies with that guidance.

4. *Unpublished guidance*

The Bill should, however, only give the proposed special status to *published* guidance.[1] There would be a danger of distortion of competitive conditions if one firm were able to rely on unpublished guidance when other firms cannot. In addition, giving special status to unpublished guidance could unjustifiably affect third party rights by prejudicing legitimate expectations.[2] The Government has already stated that the FSA should be required to publish for consultation any standing guidance that it proposes to issue.[3]

5. *Requirements to issue guidance*

We do not advocate that the FSA should be compelled to issue guidance on request. As the Government has stated, this could place a considerable burden on the regulator.[4] However, powers to issue guidance are of no value unless they are used. In particular, the FSA should be willing to issue published guidance in individual cases as a means of developing policy and responding to particular situations.

6. *Proposed amendments*

6.1   We propose that the draft Bill should be amended by the addition of the following provisions:

(1)   A person is taken to act in conformity with any rule or any statement of principles prepared or issued under this Act or any other requirement which is imposed by or under this Act and whose contravention does not constitute an offence[5], where the Authority has published guidance on compliance with that rule, statement or requirement and, in reliance on the standards set out in that guidance, that person believes on reasonable grounds that he is acting in conformity with that rule, statement or requirement.

(2)   A person is taken not to have engaged in market abuse[6] or other conduct for which a fine may be imposed under section 58 of this Act[7] where the Authority has published guidance to the effect that certain conduct does not constitute market abuse or such other conduct and, in reliance on the standards set out in that guidance, that person believes on reasonable grounds that his conduct does not constitute market abuse or such other conduct.

(3)   Where the Authority has published guidance on compliance with any requirement which is imposed by or under this Act and whose contravention constitutes an offence, compliance with that guidance may be relied on as tending to establish that:

(a)   in relation to any offence where this would be a defence, a person took all reasonable precautions and exercised all due diligence to avoid committing the offence;

(b)   in relation to any contravention of such a requirement where this is relevant for the purposes of this Act, a person reasonably believed that he or another relevant person was not contravening that prohibition;[8] and

---

[1]   Clause 87(3)(a) contemplates that the FSA may, but is not required to, publish its guidance.

[2]   Compare for example the treatment of unpublished guidance under the Competition Act 1998.

[3]   Paragraph 5.4 of HM Treasury Progress Report.

[4]   Paragraph 5.8 of HM Treasury Progress Report.

[5]   See e.g., clause 43 (need for approval), paragraph 18 of Schedule 3 (exercise of passport rights by UK firms), newly published clause A3 (restrictions on promotion of collective investment schemes).

[6]   Market abuse does not fall within (1) above as the draft Bill does not propose to impose a "requirement" not to engage in market abuse.

[7]   Our submission to HM Treasury suggested that the provisions of section 58(b) were in fact unduly broad. It would give the FSA power to fine anyone for "taking action or refraining from taking action that has induced another person or persons to engage in market abuse". This might be used to fine someone who gives advice on the market abuse regime (even where that advice is not negligent) or someone who is not under any duty to take any action to dissuade someone else from engaging in market abuse.

[8]   See below.

(c) in relation to an offence under section 212(3), a person reasonably believed that his act or conduct would not create an impression that was false or misleading as to the matters mentioned in that section.

6.2 The provision in (1) above is modelled on existing provisions in the FSA's own rulebook and the rulebooks of the self-regulating organisations.

6.3 Failure to comply with guidance should not, however, tend to establish that defences are not available or tend to establish *non-compliance* with applicable rules, etc. The FSA should not have the power, in effect, to extend the criminal law or its own rules without compliance with the appropriate statutory procedures.

7. *Related matters*

7.1 The Bill should give the court power to allow the enforcement of a contract resulting from unlawful financial promotion where the person seeking to enforce the contract reasonably believed that he had not contravened the prohibition on financial promotion.[1]

7.2 The provisions on financial promotion and the provisions relating to the authorisation offence should allow a person to enforce a contract entered into as a result of unlawful activity by a third party at least where the person seeking to enforce did not know of the contravention by the third party or reasonably believed that the third party was not contravening the relevant prohibition.[2] It would in fact be more consistent to specify that a person should be entitled to enforce his contract where he was not knowingly concerned in the contravention of the Act by a third party.[3]

7.3 The Bill should be reviewed to ensure that all relevant offences have either a "due diligence defence" or a "reasonable belief" defence.[4]

7.4 The FSA's powers to give guidance should be extended to cover guidance on related statutory provisions such as the insider dealing legislation, public offers of securities regulations and money laundering regulations and FSA guidance should be given similar status in relation to those provisions as well.

28 April 1999

APPENDIX 7

Memorandum from Mr Guy Morton, partner, Freshfields

I do not think that I can usefully add anything further to the debate on the ECHR, but I do have one more general comment on the Treasury memorandum. This relates to paragraph 15, which I read as saying that the Government does not intend to make any change to the drafting of the basic definition of "market abuse" in clause 56 of the Bill. If my interpretation is right, I find this disappointing; for the reasons which I explained to the Joint Committee, I remain of the view that clause 56 in its current from does not give a sufficiently clear impression of what conduct is regarded a objectionable. The proposed changes outlined in paragraph 16 of the memorandum are very welcome, but do not seem to me entirely to cure the problem.

21 May 1999

APPENDIX 8

Joint Memorandum from the British Bankers' Association and the Association of British Insurers

1. INTRODUCTION

1.1 The Association of British Insurers and the British Bankers' Association welcome the invitation of the Joint Committee to comment on the Treasury Memorandum on Human Rights Issues raised by the draft Financial Services and Markets Bill. The comments below are made in the light of the Treasury Memorandum and of the comments made by the Economic Secretary to the Treasury and Counsel in evidence to the Joint Committee on 19 May.

1.2 The proposals set out by the Treasury provide safeguards for those suspected of market abuse and are a welcome step towards allaying our concerns that the draft Bill could be incompatible with the European Convention on Human Rights (ECHR). We believe that the FSA should provide equivalent safeguards for those

---

[1] Compare clause 19 with clause 16(4)(b).
[2] Compare clause 16(4)(c) and section 5(3)(b) of the Financial Services Act 1986.
[3] Compare Part XVIII of the draft Bill and in particular clauses 202(2) and (3), 204(1) and 206(1).)
[4] See e.g., clause 120(8).

involved in internal disciplinary proceedings to ensure that a challenge on human rights grounds cannot be sustained, a possibility which would bring the FSA's authority into disrepute.

1.3   It will still, however, be important to draw a distinction between criminal proceedings, the exercise of the FSA's market abuse fining power and the internal disciplinary process so that the last, in particular, does not become overly legalistic in a way which inhibits the FSA's ability to regulate effectively by making it incapable of delivering speedy decisions at an acceptable cost.

2.   MARKET ABUSE

2.1   The new civil power to fine for market abuse is additional to the existing criminal offences of insider dealing and market manipulation. We note that the Treasury recognises there is a possibility that the market abuse fining power may be classified as criminal for Convention purposes and are pleased to see that the Treasury is proposing changes to the Bill to ensure compliance with the ECHR.

2.2   We welcome the intention to explore providing subsidised legal assistance in appropriate cases. It is not entirely clear from the Treasury's Memorandum whether such assistance will be available in both market abuse and disciplinary actions and we would welcome confirmation that it is the intention to cover all hearings before the Tribunal.

2.3   We also welcome the intention that compliance with the Code of Market Conduct will be an absolute defence against proceedings for breach of the market abuse legislation. We would encourage the Government also to introduce explicit protection for people who take reasonable steps not to breach the primary provisions, which, as noted in the Progress Report (13.7), do not by themselves provide sufficient certainty as to the application of the regime.

We would also encourage the FSA to provide the same assurance that those who have complied with specific rules, codes and guidance will not be pursued for alleged breaches of the FSA's Principles for authorised and approved persons.

2.4   There is as yet no definition proposed for "market participant", although there was discussion at the hearing on 19 May of the scope of the definition. In particular, the extent to which off-market activity is intended to be caught needs to be clarified, as does the concept of abuse by inaction set out in Clause 58(b) of the draft Bill. As organisations representing major investors and traders, we recognise the importance of maintaining the high reputation of the markets and protecting legitimate activities. Therefore, provided adequate safeguards against abuse of the regime are in place, we would welcome a definition sufficiently wide to encompass all active market participants.

3.   DISCIPLINE

3.1   We note the Government view that the disciplinary provisions of the Bill are likely to be classified as the determination of civil rights and obligations for the purposes of the Bill. In our view, the arguments put forward by the Government put too much weight on the restricted community involved and do not take into account the way in which a disciplinary fine on an individual can effectively deprive them of the ability to earn a living in their chosen field. Whatever the eventual classification of this regime, we consider that the disciplinary regime adopted by the FSA should be compatible with basic standards of fairness and with the ECHR.

3.2   Proceedings under the discipline provisions are essentially administrative in nature, and it is important that the process should be accessible in terms of both process and cost. Individuals may need more protection than large firms. The challenge faced by the FSA is to put in place a process that meets both the requirements for certainty and simplicity. One possibility would be to require the Treasury to provide guidance on the fairness of the FSA processes.

3.3   The penalties imposed should be proportionate both to the nature of the offence and the circumstances of the accused. We welcome the clarification that non-payment of a fine will not punishable by imprisonment.

3.4   We further note that the use of compelled evidence under the disciplinary regime is unclear. If disciplinary proceedings are considered to be civil in nature, compelled evidence will be admissible at the stage of consideration by the Enforcement Committee. If the Tribunal is considering a criminal case, the Treasury Memorandum makes it clear that such evidence is inadmissible. However, if a disciplinary case is referred to the Tribunal, operating as an Administrative Tribunal, it is unclear whether compelled evidence could be used. Clearly, if it is not admissible, there will be a strong incentive for those accused of disciplinary offences to take cases to the Tribunal, which will reduce the likelihood of settlement at earlier stages, and add to the cost and time involved in the process.

21 May 1999

APPENDIX 9

Memorandum from the London Investment Banking Association

1. The Members of the London Investment Banking Association (LIBA) very much support the objectives set out by the Treasury in their memorandum: the regulatory system to be established under the Bill must be clear, robust and effective but the system must also be fair and fully protective of human rights. We must emphasise that we share the Government's view that high standards should be expected of financial services firms—our concern is that the legislation should ensure a fair disciplinary process.

2. In this letter we comment on the main issue raised in the Clerk's letter to us of 14 May, namely whether the proposals in the Treasury's Memorandum make it more likely that the eventual legislation will be free from challenge on human rights grounds. As explained, below, we believe that the Treasury's proposals—although helpful in the Market Abuse area—are insufficient. We would also note the concerns we have expressed earlier about the rationale for the introduction of a new "civil" offence and there continue to be many concerns about the way the offence is currently drafted.[1]

MARKET ABUSE

3. We are pleased that the Government has decided to put in place new safeguards designed to ensure that ECHR protections are enshrined in the Market Abuse legislation proposed in the draft Bill. Apart from the announced changes to the Enforcement Committee/Tribunal process we believe that the three key elements[2] which need to be included are protection against the use of compelled statements, the provision of legal assistance to those who do not have sufficient means, and amendments to the framework proposed in the draft Bill to achieve the Article 7 requirement for certainty.

4. Our understanding is that the legislation will be amended to provide for the first two of these and that, on the third, the Government:

   (1) proposes to make compliance with express provisions in the FSA Code an absolute defence against proceedings for breach of the Market Abuse provisions (we assume that this will entail an amendment to Clause 57 of the draft Bill);

   (ii) proposes to clarify in the Bill that the Market Abuse regime will only apply to "market participants";

   (iii) will consider the introduction of explicit protections for people who take reasonable steps to make sure that they do not breach the primary provisions (again we assume that this will entail amendments to the Bill).

5. We believe that these proposals are extremely helpful and that they could address most of the concerns that we and other bodies have raised on the certainty issue with regard to the Market Abuse offence.

6. Until drafts of the provisions are brought forward, however, our view on whether they will suffice to enable the Market Abuse legislation to stand up to legal challenge on ECHR grounds is cautious. In particular, we continue to believe that a mental element is needed in the definition of the offence—we are not sure that point (ii) above will achieve this satisfactorily—and we are unclear how "market participant" will be defined (point (iii) above). We also continue to believe that the Code should recognise that compliance with an exchange rule should also provide a defence against a Market Abuse charge.

7. Moreover, the value of point (i) above in achieving the necessary certainty will depend on the extent of revisions to the Market Abuse Code proposed in FSA's consultation paper 10: in particular, it will be necessary for the Code to make clear what behaviour is held to be unacceptable and the Code will need to cover all aspects of the statutory offence if areas of uncertainty are not to remain. We would draw the Committee's attention, in particular, to our concerns about the unclear and subjective tests in the current drafting of Clauses 56(1)(c) and 58(b) and to the lack of clarity about the "in relation to" tests in Clauses 56(4) and (5).

8. Until the overall package of measures covering Market Abuse can be reviewed, therefore, we believe that it is not possible to confirm that the new proposals in themselves will protect the FSA from successful challenges under the Convention. It would undoubtedly be helpful in this regard, however, if the Government was to make it clear that it intended to address the above concerns.

---

[1] See our submission to the Joint Committee of 21 April and our submission to the Treasury of 16 November in which we raised a number of concerns about the drafting of Clauses 56 and 58(2): we suggested that strengthening the existing criminal offences might be a better way forward. In our submission to the Treasury on the draft Bill we also raised concerns about consultation and accountability: in particular, whilst Clauses 57(8)–(10) require consultation on the Market Abuse Code, there appears to be no requirement for consultation on subsequent amendments to it (Clause 57(4)). Given the subject matter, it is essential that market practitioners' views are taken into account before the Code—or amendments to it—are promulgated.

[2] We understand that the Government will be responding to the Joint Committee's recommendations on the payment of compensation (paragraph 146 of the First Report; and also see paragraphs 10 and 11 of the Joint Opinion of Lord Lester and Javan Herberg of 27 October 1998).

FSA'S DISCIPLINARY PROCESS

9. The memorandum explains that the Government believes that FSA's disciplinary process should not be regarded as "criminal" for the purposes of the Convention and therefore no changes to the Bill are proposed in this area. The fact that eminent lawyers have differing views indicates that the arguments on this matter appear to be finely balanced—as we discuss below—and we are very concerned at the risk that the FSA's disciplinary process will be vulnerable to successful challenge if the new framework does not provide Convention safeguards. This could be potentially very serious for the efficacy of the new regime and, since inclusion of the three key safeguards set out in paragraph 3 above would not appear to undermine FSA's disciplinary process, we believe that the prudent course, given the prevailing uncertainty, would be to proceed on the basis that the process—at least in certain cases—should be regarded as potentially criminal for ECHR purposes.

10. It may be that amendments to the legislation are not essential for this: for example, perhaps the same result could be achieved if FSA made completely clear in its forthcoming policy statement that the disciplinary process would reflect Convention safeguards, and this policy was endorsed by the Government. However, it is not clear to us that such a non-legislative solution would protect FSA from successful challenge. Given that there appear to be good arguments on both sides as to whether particular conduct the subject of the disciplinary regime will be regarded as criminal or civil in ECHR terms, we believe that perhaps a way forward is for it to be made clear in the legislation where the line is to be drawn. In achieving this, the law should err on the side of caution to avoid the risk of a Court determining at some later date that safeguards, which were not provided, should have been. This would enable the "compatibility statement" to be made under Section 19 of the Human Rights Act to be given with complete assurance.

Practical implications of recognising the ECHR safeguards

11. Perhaps the most important Convention safeguard as far as the day-to-day business of firms is concerned is the principle that behaviour should not result in punishment unless the prospect of the behaviour resulting in disciplinary sanction is reasonably foreseeable when it is undertaken. This issue will largely arise in practice in the context of whether FSA should be able to take disciplinary action—i.e., the imposition of a fine or public censure of a firm—for breaches of the Principles alone. We consider that the issue of uncertainty will only arise in respect of those Principles which are drafted in the most general and/or subjective terms. Thus introduction of the "certainty safeguard" would only be of practical significance if there are Principles which do not indicate the sorts of behaviour which is considered to be unacceptable,. We do not believe that the introduction of the certainty safeguard would in practice have the effect of curtailing FSA's ability to *police* firms' behaviour—it would only limit the ability to *punish* on the rare occasions when an abuse occurs which is not otherwise covered in the rules or guidance. When such a new abuse was detected the firm would be required to cease that behaviour and a specific rule introduced to permit punishment of anybody else who repeated the abuse. In this connection we would note that it appears to be common ground that Convention safeguards—if they are required—would only be applicable to FSA's exercise of its *disciplinary* powers and would not apply to the exercise of the powers of intervention,

The legal arguments

12. As for the legal arguments, we must defer to the lawyers whose Opinions the Joint Committee has already received. We would note, however, that although the underlying purpose of providing FSA with disciplinary powers is to provide protection, as the Treasury argue, the mechanism for delivering this objective is to deter behaviour in breach of the rules through the imposition of significant penalties. The third sentence of paragraph 11 of the Treasury's memorandum appears to confirm the importance of severe penalties for the deterrence element, and our understanding of the advice provided by Lord Lester is that this is the key test in determining whether the regime should be regarded as criminal for ECHR purposes. We would also note that our understanding of the cases referred to by the Treasury is that these primarily concern the ability of professional bodies to determine whether a person should be able to act in a professional capacity and that they do not deal with the imposition of fines solely for deterrence purposes. We accept that procedures with regard to the former may not be regarded as criminal for Convention purposes but the fundamental question is whether a framework which allows for the imposition of unlimited fines for punitive and deterrent purposes would be regarded as criminal under the Convention or not.[1]

13. We would note, in addition, that the Treasury's memorandum does not comment on the recent French judgment—in the *Oury* case—where it appears to have been accepted by the French Appeal Court that the Convention's criminal safeguards should apply. Lord Lester has explained the relevance of this case, most recently in his memorandum of 18 May to the Joint Committee. While Mr Kentridge spoke to the Committee about the case, he dealt with only one of the two *Oury* judgments. The second judgment, which dealt with composition of the body which reached the enforcement decision of the Commission des Operations de Bourse (COB) is perhaps more relevant. FSA's consultation paper 17 highlights that a major purpose of the disciplinary

---

[1] The Treasury's memorandum also observes that there is no provision for imprisonment in default of payment of a fine: for fines imposed on firms, of course, the question of imprisonment does not arise.

process is to impose sanctions for deterrent and punitive purposes—see for example paragraphs 82 and 104 of CP 17—and the similar approach by the COB was important in the determination that the sanctions available to the French regulator were criminal in nature.

14. In addition, and as we have argued previously, we believe that providing Convention safeguards is important in ensuring the fairness of FSA's process whether or not, in strict law, the disciplinary process should be regarded as criminal for ECHR purposes: we do not believe—as noted above—that the introduction of such safeguards would undermine the efficacy of FSA's policing powers.

COMPLIANCE WITH RULES: NO ACTION PROCEDURES

15. In the Market Abuse context, the Government proposes to make compliance with the FSA Code a defence against proceedings. We believe that a similar approach should be adopted by FSA with regard to disciplinary proceedings for breaches of their Principles so that compliance with a specific rule should protect a firm against disciplinary action for breach of a Principle (this would build on the Joint Committee's recommendation at paragraph 248 in the First Report of last month). In addition, we feel that we should also point out that another way of providing certainty to firms is by amending the legislation so as to allow them to obtain guidance from FSA on the legitimacy of transactions under the rules: if, ultimately, it is decided that Convention safeguards should not apply to FSA's disciplinary process, we think that it will be particularly important for the Government to consider again the need for a binding no action procedure.

CONCLUSION

16. It will be clear that we have serious concerns that the proposals in the Treasury memorandum are not sufficient to ensure that the legislation will stand up to legal challenge on ECHR grounds. Moreover, we believe that the introduction of a disciplinary regime without Convention safeguards—whether or not such safeguards are legally required—will force firms to seek more detailed rules to secure the level of certainty that they need that the business which they are undertaking will not give rise to disciplinary penalties: we are concerned that this will be destructive of innovation in London's financial markets. We do not wish to limit FSA's ability to operate Principles but merely to constrain the ability to use the most subjective of the Principles—for example Principle 5 of the present draft (in consultation paper 13)—as a basis for punishment.

17. Please let us know if it would be helpful for the Joint Committee to discuss these issues with LIBA.

21 May 1999

Printed in the UK by The Stationery Office Limited
6/99   432317   78344

ISBN 0-10-406699-7

Published by The Stationery Office Limited
and available from:

The Publications Centre
(Mail, telephone and fax orders only)
PO Box 276, London SW8 5DT
General enquiries *Lo-call* 0345 58 54 63
Order through the Parliamentary Hotline *Lo-call* 0345 02 34 74
Fax orders 0171 873 8200

The Stationery Office Bookshops
123 Kingsway, London WC2B 6PQ
0171 242 6393 Fax 0171 242 6394
68-69 Bull Street, Birmingham B4 6AD
0121 236 9696 Fax 0121 236 9699
33 Wine Street, Bristol BS1 2BQ
0117 926 4306 Fax 01179 294515
9-21 Princess Street, Manchester M60 8AS
0161 834 7201 Fax 0161 833 0634
16 Arthur Street, Belfast BT1 4GD
0123 223 8451 Fax 0123 223 5401
The Stationery Office Oriel Bookshop
18-19 High Street, Cardiff CF1 2BZ
01222 395548 Fax 01222 384347
71 Lothian Road, Edinburgh EH3 9AZ
0131 228 4181 Fax 0131 622 7017

The Parliamentary Bookshop
12 Bridge Street, Parliament Square,
London SW1A 2JX
Telephone orders 0171 219 3890
General enquiries 0171 219 3890
Fax orders 0171 219 3866

Accredited Agents
(see Yellow Pages)

and through good booksellers

ISBN 0 10 406699 7